THE PURPOSES OF
AMERICAN POWER

LEHRMAN INSTITUTE BOOKS

The Lehrman Institute was founded in 1972 as a private, nonprofit, operating foundation devoted to the analysis of public policy in its broadest aspects, with particular emphasis on the historical roots of contemporary policy questions. The Institute encourages interdisciplinary study — so as to foster a greater awareness of the interpretation of history, politics, and economics — and also contributes to nonpartisan debate on contemporary policy issues. To these ends, the Institute sponsors annually a program of seminars organized around the works-in-progress of a small number of Fellows and also conducts other series of study groups focusing on major problems in foreign affairs and economic policy. These seminars bring together scholars, businessmen, journalists, and public servants.

In 1976, the Institute began publishing books under its aegis that include specially commissioned essays and other monographs originally presented as working papers in Institute seminars and that, in the judgment of the Trustees of the Institute, are worthy of presentation to a wider public.

The Lehrman Institute does not take any position with regard to any issue: all statements of fact and expression of opinion in these publications are the sole responsibility of the individual authors.

THE PURPOSES OF AMERICAN POWER

An Essay on National Security

ROBERT W. TUCKER

A LEHRMAN INSTITUTE BOOK

PRAEGER SPECIAL STUDIES • PRAEGER SCIENTIFIC

Library of Congress Cataloging in Publication Data

Tucker, Robert W.
    The Purposes of American Power.

    (A Lehrman Institute book)
        1. United States—Foreign relations—1981–
2. United States—National security.   3. United States
—Foreign relations—Soviet Union.   4. Soviet Union—
Foreign relations—United States.   I. Title.   II. Series:
Lehrman Institute book.
E876.T83   327.73   81-8675
ISBN 0-03-059974-1   AACR2
ISBN 0-03-059976-8 (pbk.)

Published in 1981 by Praeger Publishers
CBS Educational and Professional Publishing
A Division of CBS, Inc.
521 Fifth Avenue, New York, New York 10175 U.S.A.
© 1981 by The Lehrman Institute

123456789   038   987654321

Printed in the United States of America

Preface

This essay was written in late 1980, against the background of rising debate over the foreign policy of the United States. Since its completion, a new administration has come to office, intent upon effecting substantial change in the policies pursued during the preceding decade. It is tempting to comment on the initial measures taken by the Reagan Administration. If that temptation has been suppressed, it is because my intention has been to analyze the principal features of foreign policy in the 1970s, to consider the general position in which we now find ourselves and to articulate the principal alternative directions that American policy might take in the years ahead. The essay should be read as a commentary written at a critical juncture in the history of the post World War II period. It may also be considered as a yardstick—one among several—against which the emerging policies of the Reagan Administration may be judged.

In one form or another, the various parts of the essay were given as seminars at the Lehrman Institute as part of the Institute's continuing interest in the area of national security. Major parts of the essay appeared in *Foreign Affairs* ("America in Decline: The Foreign Policy of 'Maturity,'" *America and the World, 1979;* "The Purposes of American Power," Winter 1980–81) and in *Commentary* ("American Power and the Persian Gulf," November 1980).

In preparing the essay for publication I was greatly helped by the efforts of David Hendrickson, Nicholas X. Rizopoulos, Linda Wrigley, and Catherine Grover. It is a pleasure to acknowledge them here.

Contents

vii

THE PURPOSES OF
AMERICAN POWER

I

A Critical Juncture

Once again we have reached a major turning point in American foreign policy. On this, at least, there is widespread agreement. The conviction that the nation has come to a critical juncture in its foreign relations is broadly shared by those who may disagree on virtually everything else. Everywhere the signs point to the conclusion that for the third time in the post-World War II period we are in the throes of far-reaching change in the nation's foreign policy. What these signs do not divulge are the eventual scope and magnitude of the change.

Yet the same was true of the two earlier occasions in which American foreign policy underwent significant transformation. The observer in 1947 could not have known the form that the emerging policy of containment would take. In its inception containment had no determinate outcome. Neither the external circumstances in which containment arose and which conditioned the immediate development of that policy, nor the domestic reaction to these circumstances, dictated the form that containment would ultimately take. It is true that in the sweeping language of the Truman Doctrine — "We must assist free peoples to work out their destinies in their own way" — as well as in its sense of universal crisis — "At the present moment in world history every nation must choose between alternative ways of life" — we can see the subsequent course of a policy that led to the equation of American security with world order, world order with the containment of communism, and the containment of communism with the conflict — Vietnam — that brought an end to the policy of global containment.

But the Truman Doctrine did not foreordain Vietnam, whatever the intent of its authors. It was the American intervention in Korea — prompted far more by conventional balance-of-power calculations than by the universal pretensions of the Truman Doctrine — that led to the extension of containment in Asia, which was divisive from the start and never supported by more than a negative consensus.

What may be said of the policy of global containment may also be said of the policy that succeeded it in the late 1960s and early 1970s. The Nixon policy reformulation held out the promise of a foreign policy that, while preserving America's essential role and interests in the world, would be far less burdensome than the policy it presumably displaced. That promise could not be fulfilled. The logic of the Nixon reformulation, with its centerpiece of detente, was the logic of retrenchment. This is not to say that the "new structure of peace" had from its inception a determinate outcome that had to lead as surely to the general decline experienced by America in the 1970s as the policy of containment had to lead to Vietnam. The retrenchment initiated by the Nixon Administration could have been curtailed well short of the limits it eventually reached by the end of the past decade, just as the containment initiated by the Truman Administration could have been curtailed short of the limits it reached by the mid-1960s.

The domestic circumstances that attended the coming to power of the Carter Administration did not dictate the foreign policy that it followed during its years in office. In contributing to the further decline in the American global position, the Carter Administration acted as much from internal conviction — not domestic political necessity — as the Johnson Administration did in its pursuit of the war in Vietnam.

It is worth recalling these earlier occasions today, if only to question the view that the course of American foreign policy in the 1980s is already largely foreclosed. This view is shared by otherwise very divergent groups in the foreign policy spectrum. It is emphasized both by those who believe we must adjust our interests and behavior to the more modest position we now occupy in the world and by those who believe we can and must recapture the position and leadership we once enjoyed. To the former, adjustment to our diminished status is a necessity we can vainly attempt to ecape only at our grave peril. To the latter, the reassertion of something akin to our former role is the only safe course we can take if we are not to suffer ever more severe threats to our security, whether in our competition with the Soviet Union or in our attempt to preserve the essential elements of a moderate international system.

If these positions are oversimplified here, the emphasis common to both is clear enough. In a darkening international landscape, the view that we must return to our pre-Vietnam role has recently gained an unexpected strength. Even so, its emphasis on the virtual absence of any other choice lacks persuasiveness. The degree of freedom in foreign policy we continue to enjoy today, once immediate security threats are addressed, may not be as broad as it once was, but it is still considerable. How this freedom will be employed remains an open question.

What is no longer open to question is the decline in the nation's power and position that has occurred in the past decade. The causes of this decline continue to elicit a great deal of controversy, but they ought not to obscure the decline itself. Even if America's eroding position were beyond our ability to alter in any significant manner — a proposition that must be rejected — this would not alter the fact of serious erosion. Though disputed until recently, it is no longer a matter of serious contention. Under the impact of events that brought the last decade to a close and ushered in the 1980s, the fact of America's decline has become a commonplace.

II

America in Decline: The 1970s

1

Political tradition has it that an administration must take responsibility for what happens in the course of its tenure. It is not surprising then, that the Carter Administration had to bear a heavy onus for the developments that occurred during its years in office. There is a kind of poetic justice at work here, for seldom in recent American history was an administration as anxious to disavow the efforts of its predecessor and to proclaim "new beginnings" as this one. Many critics with an axe to grind, or a record to defend, have equated the decline of American power with the actions of those who were so intent to mark 1977 as the start of a new era in the nation's foreign policy.

The equation, though perhaps understandable, is nevertheless false. It was not the Carter Administration that concluded the first SALT agreements, within the terms of which the Soviet Union was able by 1977 to develop the base for what may yet become a superior counterforce capability. Nor was it the Carter Administration that inaugurated detente in 1972 and claimed that in doing so it had laid the foundation of a stable and lasting structure of peace. And it was not the Carter Administration that remained passive before the first great challenge mounted by the OPEC states in 1973–74. These were the actions of the predecessors of the Carter Administration. In their effects, they compromised American interests and power to an extent we can only now fully appreciate. The Carter Administration had to contend with the consequences. If its efforts left a great deal to be desired, it still cannot be assigned exlusive responsibility for our present vulnerability to Soviet arms and Persian Gulf oil, vulnerabilities that are likely to represent the two most critical problems for American foreign policy in the years to come.

The legacy bequeathed to the Carter Administration in 1977 was already modest by comparison with what it once was. To what extent did this diminished legacy result from the actions of those responsible for the conduct of policy during the eight preceding years? Did the Nixon-Kissinger policies lead to the sacrifice of interests that might have been preserved and the compromise of positions that might have been maintained intact? Did the "new structure of peace" weaken further the domestic base of support by its sterility of purpose and its almost

8

obsessively secretive methods? The Nixon policy reformulation called for a new modesty in thought and action;
it emphasized the inherent limits to any nation's wisdom,
understanding, and energy. Yet it was not prepared to
accept a significant change in role and interests. Was
there not a contradiction between the emphasis on the
limits to our power and what we could reasonably accomplish, and the almost equal emphasis on continuity
in role and interest? Finally, was not the policy itself
flawed by virtue of the assumptions on which it apparently rested: that allies would prove reasonably passive,
adversaries reasonably restrained, and the developing
world reasonably stable and undemanding?

These questions still do not yield clear answers. Even
so, it is apparent that domestic events were very significant, perhaps even critical, for the development of a large
part of the Nixon policy. Without Watergate, the end in
Vietnam would almost surely have been quite different.
There still would have been an end that spelled American
defeat, but it would not have come with the suddenness
and brutality it did in 1975. Whether in the absence of
Watergate detente would have developed as it did is
more arguable. Still, unless one is prepared to ignore the
record of the Nixon Administration prior to 1973, it
seems only plausible to project a different outcome from
that experienced.

Domestic constraints alone, however, cannot explain
the fate of the Nixon policy reformulation and particularly its centerpiece: detente. They can neither explain the

flaws in the initial design nor account for the whole of its subsequent development over the succeeding four years. The principal question the detente of 1972 raised was this: What would induce a more moderate Soviet Union that no longer sought to exploit opportunities and take advantage of instabilities—that would, indeed, increasingly accept American inspired rules of the game"? The Nixon Administration responded that this would result from a combination of positive incentives—primarily economic—and diplomatic pressures—expressed principally in the then emergent Chinese-American relationship. Clearly, it did not simply discard the previous methods of containment. But it was equally clear that it did not accord the same role to these methods in the new policy. Had it done so, there would have been little need for the new positive incentives and diplomatic pressures upon which so much emphasis was placed and which indeed formed the core of the ostensibly novel design.

To argue otherwise in retrospect, to present the detente of 1972 as a continuation of earlier methods, now more effectively employed if only by virtue of their linkage to still other means of inducing Soviet restraint— to argue, in effect, that detente was in reality intended as a kind of supercontainment or containment-plus—does not accord with the words and certainly not with the actions of those responsible at the time for American policy. Nor is it the way to read memoirs written with an eye to tailoring the past to the political requirements of the present.* A design of containment-plus would have had to assume that in the early 1970s the United States was in a more favorable position to contain Soviet power than it had been a generation before. Moreover, even in the circumstances of 1972, the design would have defied obvious political realities at home. After 1972, in the atmosphere generated by Watergate, it could have made no sense at all.

Instead, the containment envisaged in 1972 was more optimistic than its predecessor with respect to both method and result. An emphasis on the importance of economic inducements in moderating Soviet behavior reflected the view that internal constraints would turn Soviet leadership away from an expansionist foreign policy. Even the marked growth of Soviet military power was given an optimistic interpretation. The principal expositor of detente, Henry Kissinger, found external constraints on Soviet behavior that were, it seemed, self-operating. The rough parity in power that now prevailed between the nuclear superpowers, he insisted in 1972, made the "constant jockeying for marginal advantages over an opponent" either very unrealistic or very dangerous or, more likely, both. If true, this made economic incentives held out to the Soviet Union largely

---

*As some have read the memoirs of Henry Kissinger, *White House Years* (Boston: Little, Brown, 1979). See, for example, Stanley Hoffmann, "The Case of Dr. Kissinger," *New York Review of Books,* December 6, 1979, pp. 14–29.

superfluous. At best, those incentives would only serve to insure such behavior that was in any case in the Soviet Union's interest to pursue.

It is likely that detente was the outcome of motives that were mixed and never easy to reconcile. The new version of containment that detente expressed evidently reflected the conviction that the growth of Soviet power, when taken together with what was perceived as growing reluctance at home to support a policy of global engagement, required that American interests would have to be preserved largely through other and easier means than those employed in the past. There was a measure of self-deception — perhaps even of deception — at work here since the new means afforded no assurance that they would prove effective. If not, the question persisted: What would prevent the steady concession of interests to the Soviets?

The answer may be that the Nixon-Kissinger detente was conceived, despite the manner in which it was put forth, more as a holding operation than a settled strategy. If so, it may have responded more to internal than to external constraints, and there was no need to assume that these internal constraints would remain unchanged. In any event, the practical meaning of detente would be revealed only in its implementation and, it may be argued, there was little in the Nixon record to suggest the implementation would be one-sided. Once again, though, we are brought back to the significance of Watergate, for it was Kissinger who was left to implement detente and to do so in very unfavorable circumstances.

These circumstances apart, the subsequent history of detente was also due to the unpromising methods by which the new relationship was to be implemented. Since economic means had never influenced Soviet high policy in the past, these was little reason to expect they would do so now. Nor was it ever very plausible to assume that a more effectively exploited triangular relationship might have done what economic incentives could not do. It is true that Kissinger did very little to exploit the new relationship with China. It is by no means apparent, however, that had the opening to Beijing been more imaginatively and assiduously pursued the result would have had an appreciable effect on the development of detente. In the new relationship with Washington, the Chinese had cast themselves almost entirely in a passive role. They would make no contribution to American efforts other than the contribution they were already making by virtue of their hostile position toward the Soviet Union. What was never successfully exploited was probably never there to exploit. If anything, from the start the Chinese indicated that it would be the other way around. Instead of being the exploiting party, Washington would have to act so as to fulfill Beijing's expectations. It soon became clear that this meant the policy of detente would be hostage to the Chinese relationship.

There is today little disposition to question what was only a short time ago very much the subject of controversy. Kissinger himself, one of the principal architects of detente and certainly its most articulate defender, has since become its severe critic, though the criticism is directed at what detente presumably became in the hands of the Carter Administration rather than what it had originally been. But what it was at its inception is, as we have seen, no easy matter to determine. What can be said with some assurance concerns the consequences to which the detente of 1972 has led. They are clearly not the consequences projected at the time by its architects. Although defended by the secretary of state until late 1975, the policy reformulation of the early 1970s was by then a failure when judged by the expectations initially entertained.

During his last year in office, Kissinger all but acknowledged the failure. He did so by his effort—his last defense—to equate detente with the prevention of nuclear war between the superpowers; when this failed to persuade, he emphasized that "the problem of our age is how to manage the emergence of the Soviet Union as a superpower." This emphasis was not to be taken at face value since the problem had been with us since the 1940s. Instead, it was an admission that earlier expectations had not materialized and that, in consequence, the outlook and strategy that had informed the policy of detente would have to be seriously altered or abandoned.

But if this were so, there was no escape from the attempt to refashion containment in a manner that would deal more effectively with the problems posed by the startling growth of Soviet military power. The great problem that had confronted Nixon and Kissinger in 1969 was passed on, in worsened form, to their successors. To it would have to be added the challenge from the Persian Gulf.

These considerations must be balanced by recalling the adverse domestic circumstances of the years in question. Any judgment of the Kissinger period must take into account the difficulties marking his tenure. Half of these years were taken up by a war that presented only risks. Nor could these risks be readily turned aside without the prospect of incurring other, and possibly graver, risks. Even if the argument is granted that the war was needlessly prolonged, its earlier settlement would not have been on better terms and could not have avoided the broad consequences attending defeat.

The years immediately following the war were marked by growing dissension over the course American foreign policy should take. The real breakdown of the foreign policy consensus, particularly among the elites, occurred during the mid-1970s. This fact alone made the conduct of policy a difficult task. To it, however, must be added the effects of Watergate. Whatever the deeper meaning of that traumatic event, its effects on the conduct of foreign policy are not in doubt. A distracted, then paralyzed president was followed by an appointed president whose powers in foreign affairs were substantially circumscribed by Congress. The institution that had forged America's global position had lost its former dominance.

Thus the years marking Kissinger's clear ascendancy as the guiding force of American foreign policy were years during which the domestic base was weaker than it had been at any time since the period preceding World War II. Nor was this all. The principal defects that were increasingly found in Kissinger's policies by 1975–76 had at one time been viewed as virtues. It was an indication that time had overtaken these policies and that by 1976 the domestic base to which they had once responded was in the process of reformation. The waters of Vietnam and even of Watergate were slowly beginning to recede. What remained unclear was how far the recession would go and what a new administration might do with the changing situation.

2

One of the many ironies of recent American history is that the 1976 election brought to power an administration that looked either to the recent past or to a policy-irrelevant future, while turning from office an administration that had begun to confront the present. In appearance, the contrary seemed true. Whereas Kissinger was seen by most critics as a throwback to an age the world had now moved far beyond, the Carter Administration was considered sensitive to the realities of the new world we had presumably entered. The world of Kissinger was one dominated by the "old politics" with its parochial interests, its one-way dependencies, its hierarchical ordering and marked inequalities, its obsession with equilibrium and the careful balancing of power, and its reliance on forcible methods. By contrast the world of the Carter Administration was characterized by truly global interests, by growing mutual dependencies, by far less hierarchy, by less concern with equilibrium, and by the recognition that much less reliance could be placed on the forcible methods of the past.

What impressed the new administration most was the vast change it found occurring throughout most of the world. How to play a constructive role in this change, how to get on the side of it rather than to oppose it and to suffer increasing isolation from so many nations and people, was and remained a dominant concern — perhaps *the* dominant concern — of the Carter Administration.

This concern continued to evoke uncertainty in policy. But there was little uncertainty over the transcendent importance of the concern itself and the general implications of change for the international system. The system had become far more complex and far less hierarchical. It had been transformed by the startling increase of relationships of interdependence which, once formed, could be broken only at exorbitant cost. These relationships might breed conflicts of interest, but such conflicts were rarely susceptible to the arbitrament of force because force was likely to prove more injurious to the user than nonforcible means. The principal sanction of the past no longer responded to the logic of the new world. For this reason alone, the hierarchy that formerly marked the international system could no longer have anything approximating the salience and significance it once had. The great powers could no longer expect to play their traditionally preponderant roles and to enjoy their once customary advantages.

One might have viewed such a new world and its policies with a sense of foreboding since, if believed in, it betokened a period in which conflict and disorder would be rampant precisely because of the many mutual dependencies to which the traditional instruments of order could no longer be readily applied, if applied at all. The oil crisis had afforded an example of how the new world might be expected to function if given full sway, and it was far from reassuring. Yet the Carter Administration faced the prospects of the new system with equanimity and even optimism. Whatever its disadvantages, they were apparently considered preferable to the disadvantages marking the traditional system. At any rate, there was presumably no escape from the new world.

It was this outlook that prompted the conclusion that the Carter Administration was oriented to the relevant future, in contrast to a Kissinger who remained mired in an irrelevant past. The principal policy expression of this contrast was the emphasis placed by the Carter Administration on the importance of North-South relationships. Kissinger had left office more preoccupied than ever with East-West relationships and their centrality to American policy. His successors announced their intention to alter Kissinger's priority of concerns. It was not surprising that they should do so, for it was the North-South relationship, between developed and developing countries, that appeared to fit their view. By contrast, relations with the Soviet Union were ill-accommodated to it. North-South relations evoked the need for world order politics. East-West relations were a reminder of balance-of-power politics. As such, they were a kind of atavism, increasingly at odds with the forces gaining ascendancy in the new global system.

From the perspective of 1981, who, then, looked to the past and who to the future? Was it Kissinger with his emphasis on the growth of Soviet military power and the problems this growth held for American policy? Or was it his successors with their concern to adjust policy to the requirements of the new world? Certainly the vision entertained by the Carter Administration did not afford much guidance for effectively coping with the problems at hand. In part, it did not do so because the vision responded to the experience of our recent past — Vietnam, above all — an experience officials of the Carter Administration were more than anxious not to repeat. Some had been active participants in this past and had come to repent of it. Others had been active critics and were intent upon showing by deed that their criticism had been sincere. Whatever the precise motivation at work, the future many saw as the basis for planning policy was one that was rooted in a disillusioning past.

In part, however, the vision entertained of the world was without much policy relevance because it was futuristic. The future that is relevant for policy can be little more than an extension of what is already immanent in the present. But the Carter Administration looked for grander vistas. What is saw, when it was not looking at the recent past, was a future that even if it were to materialize, carried little significance for policy in the late 1970s and early 1980s.

The vision of the Carter Administration was futuristic in another sense. The future it saw had a substantial element of the utopian, and this despite the lurid colors in which the world was drawn should we refuse to respond to the rising challenge of the developing countries. The argument ran that the North-South relationship held out great danger if the demands of the Third World were ignored, but that the relationship also held out great promise if these demands were given serious and sympathetic consideration. They could be given such consideration because they were essentially moderate in character. Provided that we acted wisely and sought to play a constructive role in the great transformation unfolding before us, there was little to fear. Rather than oppose change, as we had so often done in the past, we could instead be on the side of change. This in turn implied that conflict—at any rate, serious conflict—with the developing countries was unnecessary because the basis for an essentially harmonious relationship was already there, inherent in the relationship. Conflict, if it came, would presumably result from a willful refusal to see and to act upon this essential harmony.

20

In the apparent exemption of North-South relationships from the conflicts over wealth, power, and status that have been endemic to state relations in the past, the Carter Administration betrayed an extraordinary optimism. Were it not for this optimism, the apparent ambitiousness of administration policy would have seemed curious, coming as it did from those who placed such considerable emphasis on the limits to our power. Given these limits, how could we expect "to create a genuinely global framework," as the president's National Security Advisor, Zbigniew Brzezinski, so often and so grandly put our purpose? Yet the possibilities held out for policy appeared almost boundless. Nowhere was this more strikingly illustrated than in the administration's early hopes, and indeed expectations, that it might achieve a comprehensive settlement of the Middle East conflict. Whereas Kissinger had left office extremely skeptical of the near-term prospects for any further progress, his successors looked at the conflict and found the basis for a settlement. They had come to office with a plan for a comprehensive settlement. There was no intractable conflict here, just as there was no intractable conflict elsewhere.

Many observers have made the point that the Carter Administration was characterized above all by its good intentions. Yet it was not so much good intentions as an immoderate optimism that marked this administration. There was little indication of an awareness that the new departures in policy might, if seriously meant, entail a substantial price. Even to put the matter this way is misleading. The Carter Administration gave the impression that it *had* considered the consequence of its initiatives and that it was persuaded the price to be paid for its policies was very modest. In the new world, American leadership would still prevail. In the new world, a continuity of role and interest was assumed. Only the disagreeable, counterproductive, and morally offensive features of this role would be altered. Their place would be taken by policies and means that would give a new sense of purpose and that would respond to an idealism so long ignored or suppressed by a foreign policy that had been committed to little other than the promotion of equilibrium and stability.

Immoderate optimism much more than good intentions especially characterized that apparent lodestar of the Carter Administration's foreign policy: human rights. The point is not whether the emphasis given to human rights reflected political expediency or philosophical conviction. Very likely it reflected both, together with the desire of the administration "to do something different" in order to establish its separate identity. What was significant was the belief that here was a policy that would confer benefits at home and abroad, at little if any cost. There is almost no evidence of serious thought having been given at the outset to the conflicts arising between a human rights policy, however cautious and qualified that policy might prove in implementation, and the integrity of strategic interests to which the administration was presumably committed. It was simply assumed that there was no more than a nominal price tag attached to a human rights policy. The same may be said of the policies respecting the prevention of nuclear proliferation and the reduction of conventional arms transfers.

In its professed intention to preserve an essential continuity of role and interest, the Carter Administration appeared to remain faithful to the professed intention of its predecessors. Where it differed was in the assumption that this essential continuity could be realized at very little cost. True, the Nixon-Kissinger reformulation had also sought an essential continuity of policy though at a lower price, and this had been the key to the detente of 1972. But this easier version of containment still bore a facsimile to the original: it still was predicated on the centrality of Soviet power to American strategy and interest, and it still gave recognition to the need to contain this power (though the new means it gave emphasis to could not, and did not, live up to their promise).

The Carter Administration rejected anything resembling a return to an earlier version of containment and gave little indication of concern over the consequences to which the later and easier version had led. It seemed neither impressed nor oppressed by the continuing growth of Soviet military power. Was this due to a conviction that the United States remained militarily superior to the Soviet Union? Was it due to a belief that, even if we were no longer superior, military power was of declining utility? Or was it due to an unwillingness to face the problem until the course of events left no alternative?

Whatever the answer, the reasons given at the time for

the reduced importance of the Soviet-American relationship were clear enough. Stress was placed on the innovative potential of nations, their economic power, and their ideological appeal. When measured by these standards, the Soviet Union was not considered a serious threat. Indeed, by these standards it was scarcely even a worthy rival. This estimate was reflected in the confidence with which the Carter Administration undertook its abortive arms initiative in 1977, and the apparent equanimity with which, until 1978, it viewed Soviet policy in Africa, the Middle East, and Asia.

Even where it did seem that the administration was prepared to pay a serious price for maintaining continuity of role and interest, the appearance was deceptive. In the Middle East, the American role appeard far more ambitious than in the Kissinger period. Yet the significance of the change from Kissinger's policy of step-by-step diplomacy to Carter's policy of a comprehensive peace was not that there was now a willingness to commit American power in a manner that had been absent before. The policy of directly seeking a comprehensive settlement of the Middle East conflict reflected more than an obsessive ambition to achieve the unachievable. At root, it betrayed an unwillingness to commit American power.

It was of course recognized that even a comprehensive settlement would require some commitment of American power. Still, there was a considerable difference between the kind of commitment required by a comprehensive settlement and the kind required by a separate peace between Egypt and Israel. The policy of directly pursuing a comprehensive settlement did not simply reflect the conviction that a separate peace would eventually unravel or that it would facilitate a Soviet reentry in force into the Middle East. At a deeper level, opposition to a separate peace expressed the unwillingness to employ American power to forestall or, if necessary, to counter these consequences, along with the fear of having to counter a substantial portion of the Arab world. By contrast, a comprehensive settlement would presumably avoid this price. Though it might have to be attended by an American guarantee, the very comprehensiveness of the settlement would presumably give the guarantee little more than a pro forma character. In reconciling the various interests of the parties to the conflict, a comprehensive settlement would obviate the need for an American commitment that might prove both burdensome and dangerous. Despite the fate that subsequently pushed the Carter Administration to support a separate peace, the outlook that led to its initial championing of a comprehensive peace persisted.

Whether with respect to East-West, North-South, or even West-West relations, the general pattern was reasonably clear. The new administration was often distinguished from its predecessor by dint of its rhetoric, its manner and style, and its moralism. These differences, though significant, do not go to the substance of policy. In terms of substance, the distinction must principally be found in what the Carter Administration was willing to risk in blood and treasure to achieve its foreign policy objectives. The brief answer is that it was willing to risk considerably less than its predecessors had been willing to risk.

3

By the beginning of 1980, it had become clear that the Carter Administration's foreign policy was a failure. It was a failure even by its own admission. In proposing a five-year expansion of American defense forces—an expansion that responded to insistent demands of Senate defense critics who made increased military spending a condition for approval of the SALT treaty—Carter declared that "not every instance of the firm application of power is a potential Vietnam."* Such a judgment would not have been made by the president in 1977 or, for that matter, in 1978. It was, in fact, almost a paraphrase of a statement Kissinger had made in 1976, shortly before leaving office.

Even more striking was the December 1979 testimony of Secretary of Defense Harold Brown in support of the administration's proposal for increased defense expenditures. The change, Brown noted, reflected an appreciation that "we are in for a long pull in adversary relationships," and not necessarily with the Soviet Union alone.

---

*Address to Business Council executives, Washington, D.C., December 12, 1979; *New York Times,* December 13, 1979, pp. A1, 24.

"We must decide now," the secretary warned,

> whether we intend to remain the strongest nation in the world. Or we must accept now that we will let ourselves slip into inferiority, into a position of weakness in a harsh world where principles unsupported by power are victimized, and that we will become a nation with more of a past than a future.*

Most remarkable, perhaps, was Carter's public declaration in the wake of the Soviet invasion of Afghanistan. Conceding that he now saw what he had not seen before, Carter stated that his opinion of the Soviets had changed more drastically in a week than in his previous three years as president. These and similar declarations by administration officials—whatever the political pressures that brought them forth—come perhaps as close to a mea culpa as it is possible for a government to come.

The Carter Administration's foreign policy was a failure not so much because it did not succeed in resolving the great problems of American foreign policy, but because until its last year in office it had not squarely addressed these problems. It was only in late 1979 that the dangers arising from the continued rapid growth of Soviet military power were freely conceded, and then largely as a result of the debate engendered over the SALT treaty. Equally, it was only in late 1979 that the na-

---

*Testimony before the Senate Armed Services Committee, December 13, 1979; *New York Times,* December 14, 1979, pp. A1,6.

tion's vital interest in retaining access to the oil of the Persian Gulf was acknowledged for the fragile thing that it is, and then largely as a result of an event — the Iranian revolution — that revealed in almost blinding light the extent of our vulnerability. Finally, it was only in 1979 that the first serious measures were taken to correct a chronic condition of global monetary instability, and then largely as a result of the belated realization that if the United States would no longer accept responsibility for monetary stability with all that this entails, the days of the dollar as a reserve currency might soon come to an end. That the Carter Administration did not make these problems the central concerns of policy until events finally forced it to do so is as good a test as any of its failure.

There has been no dearth of criticism of the previous administration's policies. On the whole, however, this criticism has failed to enlighten. If anything, it has often served to obscure the causes of failure. The criticism that the Carter Administration erred in trying to do too much too soon merely obscures the matter if it does not ask why it was that this administration tried to do certain things that were of secondary importance while avoiding problems that were, and remain, of prime significance. More substantial is the criticism that the Carter Administration lacked a strategic rationale and that, in the absence of such a rationale, policy remained fragmented and incoherent.

Is this view well taken? Was the apparent drift in policy due to the absence of a strategic rationale, or was it rather due to a strategic rationale that did not work? The distinction is no mere quibble. If the administration indeed lacked from the outset a strategic rationale, it is difficult to see how it can be said even to have had a foreign policy in any meaningful sense. Yet it evidently had one whatever we may think of it. If policy and strategic rationale were subject to varying interpretations by administration officials, this is testimony only to the fact that there were those who became increasingly restive over both. At that, the seriousness of opposition to the prevailing contours of policy is easily exaggerated. At the outset there certainly was no apparent division of real import. If division eventually developed, it is not so much because of the administration's admittedly unusual style of policymaking as it is that the failure of policy often generates serious divisions within any government.

Whether one takes the position that there was no strategic rationale or the position that there was such a rationale and that it suffered the fate of policy, the same question would arise: What accounts for either the absence or the failure? Clearly, one answer is the world view entertained by the administration on coming to office, a view that apparently continued to claim the allegiance of a majority of its policymakers. The world did not conform to this view. Instead of the emergence of a new politics we found ourselves still very much enmeshed in the old politics. In this familiar world, the overall stakes of superpower rivalry remained largely unchanged from the stakes of a generation ago.

There were, to be sure, changes that occurred in the respective positions of the contenders. Whereas a generation ago the United States was still in its period of youthful exuberance, by the late 1970s it had presumably entered a period of "maturity." The former aspiration to preside over and give direction to change in developing countries was succeeded by the desire to find a way by which we might get on the side of change we no longer aspired to control, or believed we could control even if we so aspired. Whereas a generation ago the United States enjoyed a marked advantage over the Soviet Union in the means of carrying on the competition in the Third World, by the late 1970s this advantage had considerably narrowed. But these significant differences notwithstanding, the rivalry itself remained very much the same. To the extent the rivalry had changed, it was chiefly because that in an increasingly resource-hungry world the stakes had become all the more serious.

Nor is it the case that the old politics must be at least partially abandoned because those who were once the largely passive objects of superpower rivalry are no longer so. Certainly the peoples of the developing countries are no longer characterized by the passivity they once displayed. But this change has prompted the superpowers to alter their methods of competition for power and influence in the Third World, not to abandon this competition.

Even then, the nature of the change when compared with a generation ago is easily exaggerated. Although we then enjoyed a relative power position we no longer have today, we nevertheless sought to contain Soviet expansion and to insure stability through the strengthening and support of friendly regional powers. In the Nixon-Kissinger period, this strategy was endowed with greatly increased significance due to the recession of American power. The Nixon Doctrine of 1969 made it a central feature in the new policy reformulation. It remained the favored strategy of the Carter Administration, all the more so given the continued erosion of American power. The hazards of heavy reliance upon it as a substitute for American power also remained, as the case of Iran so vividly demonstrated.

In a still broader sense, the growing assertiveness of the developing countries cannot be found to herald the beginning of a new world; it must be seen as the completion of the old world. What we find in the demands of the developing countries is not a challenge to the essential structure of the international system, but a challenge to the distribution of wealth and power within this system. It is not the state system per se that is condemned, but the manner in which the system operated in the past and presumably continues to operate today. It is primarily through the state that the historically oppressed and disadvantaged nations seek to mount a successful challenge to what their governing elites view as persisting inequalities. These inequalities are defined primarily in collective terms. It is not individual inequality that forms the gravamen of the indictment brought by the developing countries against the developed states but collective inequality. The greater measure of collective equality demanded does not insure a greater measure of individual equality. In the new order, as in the old, states are both the agents and subjects of equality, just as they are the agents and subjects of justice generally.

Thus the challenge of the Third World is one made by states and on behalf of states. As such, it is altogether traditional, and this is so whether it is considered in terms of the claimants or the claims. If North-South relations, and the challenge implicit in those relations, are nevertheless found to represent something that is new, the novelty must come from the number of claimants and from what is commonly seen as the growing power they represent. But these features scarcely bear out the case for the singularity with which North-South relations have been seen. Even less do they support the view that the sudden completion of the old world—with all the attendant dangers this completion holds out—requires a foreign policy that no longer operates within the categories of the past.

Why did the Carter Administration persist in the attempt to fashion a foreign policy that would presumably transcend both the limits of the old politics and the problems the old politics necessarily impose? Are we dealing here with the tyranny of intellectual fashion, a tyranny that has been so pervasive in the past decade that it finally found expression in policy? If so, the further question arises: Why was intellectual error in foreign policy so fashionable in the 1970s? The answer cannot simply be that in the past decade the complexity of the world was such as to promote error. The world did not suddenly become complex in the 1970s. Many of the characteristics of the new world that were discovered in the 1970s might have been discovered in the 1960s or even the 1950s. Yet they were discovered and converted into common currency only in the 1970s.

The reason for this is that failure is often the cause of serious reflection. The great failure of the 1960s, Vietnam, led to a widespread attack upon the intellectual rigidities that marked the period of the cold war. It led men to discover those transforming changes that were taking place before their eyes, but to which they had been largely blind because of the rigidity of thought induced by the cold war. The more important result was to create the obsessive desire that the great failure of the 1960s never be repeated. That desire could not possibly be insured without far-reaching changes in policy. As long as the United States retained an essential continuity of role and interest in the world—that is, as long it retained its position of primacy—further interventions always remained a real prospect. Either the role had to be abandoned or the prospect had to be accepted.*

The result of reflection, however, was to avoid choosing either course. Instead, a world was created in which the American role might be preserved while the former

---

*Of course, there are interventions and interventions. The desire to escape further Vietnams is one thing; the desire to escape further interventions quite another. One great difficulty of post-Vietnam policy was the failure to make this distinction.

dangers and hardships that attended this role might be avoided. We can find the beginnings of this delusion in the Nixon-Kissinger policy reformulation. The false message conveyed by detente was that what we did not wish to do — or at least some of the things we did not wish to' do — need not be done. The Carter Administration gave this message its full flowering. Reflection not only showed that what the Carter Administration did not wish to do need not be done, but that to do it would be entirely counterproductive to the nation's role and interests. In the beginning, with Nixon and Kissinger, the wish had been father to what was still a moderate thought. Now the thought — that is, the new politics — was no longer moderate because desire had markedly grown in the intervening period.

The nature of that desire was to avoid confrontations of power, especially confrontations that raised the distinct prospect of employing military power. Given this object of desire, the prevailing analyses of international politics in the past decade may be seen as the expected responses to it, for they almost invariably had the effect of confirming desire. Their common feature was that the defining characteristic of the old politics has an ever diminishing significance in the new world, and that those who failed to grasp this critical change were prisoners of a past that bore no more than peripheral relevance to the present.

The policy expressions of desire were no less apparent than desire itself. How else may one account for a defense establishment that, according to expert consensus, was considered incapable of preserving Western interests in the Persian Gulf? The prospect that this need might arise had existed for most of the 1970s. If we were incapable of vindicating our interests by force six years ago, as it was then commonly argued, there was time to remedy the vulnerability. Instead, the time was used only to increase the vulnerability. At the outset, the prevailing response to our predicament was simply to deny its reality. It could scarcely have been otherwise, else there was no alternative but to do what we persistently refused to do.

Our recent experience in the Persian Gulf also provides some insight into the likely consequences of the attempt to get on the side of change. There was nothing novel in the desire of the Carter Administration to place itself on the side of the great changes it found taking place in the developing world. Earlier administrations—the Nixon Administration excepted—professed a similar desire. The desire, whatever one may think of it, is understandable given the image we persist in entertaining of ourselves as a revolutionary society, and one whose experience we assume must be relevant to nations and peoples everywhere. Moreover, desire becomes a virtual need once the change occurring in the developing world is equated with "history." We must get on the side of change and identify with it, or else suffer isolation and become historically irrelevant.

Did this emphasis spring from a commitment to change, including revolutionary change, that was novel to the Carter Administration? In some measure it did. In the main, however, what gave rise to the new tolerance was something much less grand than philosophical conviction. It was the desire to escape from the horns of the familiar dilemma that arose out of the great failure of the 1960s, a dilemma that time and the relative erosion of American power only served to sharpen.

Politics, like other forms of behavior, has a pathology. Its symptoms are relatively clear. They consist in the refusal to confront reality (hence also in the attempts, often ingenuous, to create a reality that responds to desire), in the voluntary concession of power, and in the persuasion that all the while role and interests are being preserved. When judged by these characteristic symptoms, what was at work in American foreign policy throughout much of the preceding decade was a political pathology.

The prime symptom of this pathology was the belief that the drastic decline in American power witnessed since the late 1960s was all but inevitable. The theme that initially gained currency well over a decade ago in reaction to what was judged to be the misuse of American power became the received wisdom of the 1970s. In the process, what began as a salutory admonition on the limits to this or to any nation's power became a virtual catechism, endlessly invoked to instruct those who persisted in the error of questioning whether the course of

American policy might have been substantially different from what it was. It is this catechism on the limits to power that expressed the true spirit and inner wisdom of the Carter Administration's foreign policy of "maturity."

III

The Significance of the Present Debate

1

How are we to account for the rising debate over American foreign policy? The question itself provokes controversy. To some, the debate has been largely precipitated by domestic critics who, after several years of persistent effort, have succeeded in creating the requisite atmosphere for disaffection and debate over the nation's foreign policy. This is the view expressed most notably by former Secretary of State Cyrus Vance. To Vance, "much of the current dissatisfaction with the world and our role in it rests on certain fallacies." Those who have purveyed these fallacies or myths—above all, "the pervasive fallacy that America could have the power to order the world just the way we want it to be"—have led the way not only to much of the current dissension over foreign policy, but also to the "disturbing fear in the land that we are no longer capable of shaping our future."*

The difficulty with this view is not so much its curious portrayal of "the current dissatisfaction" as it is the inversion of cause and effect. If there has been marked dissatisfaction over American foreign policy it is not in the main the handiwork of critics but the result of events. The evidence points to the conclusion that in the absence of these events there was no real prospect of substantial change in American policy. The efforts of critics of this policy would have remained as barren of effect as they had been in years past. It has been the visible decline of American power and position that has led today to a greater dissatisfaction over foreign policy than we have experienced for a decade.

2.

If there can be little question over what has precipitated renewed debate, there can also be little question over what the debate is essentially about: American security. Once again, we are "reconsidering" our security. Moreover, we are doing so against the background of an experience that led to the discrediting of the security rationale on which postwar American foreign policy had come to

---

*Speech delivered by Cyrus Vance at Harvard University, June 5, 1980; *New York Times,* June 6, 1980, p. A12.

rest. The debate provoked by Vietnam was, like the debates of the 1930s and 1940s, a debate over security. At issue was a broad disparity of views over the conditions and the very meaning of American security interests whose vindication would justify the use of American military power. But the outcome of this debate was unlike the outcome of earlier debates. Whereas earlier debates had resulted in the triumph of the view entertained by the administration of the day, Vietnam led to the defeat of the view urged by the Johnson Administration.

The assumption that formed the core of the Johnson Administration's rationale for the American commitment in Vietnam equated the nation's security with the purpose and objectives of the Truman Doctrine and, in consequence, with the policy of global containment. What was at stake in Vietnam, the administration's argument ran, was nothing less than the principles on which the peace of the world was to be organized and maintained. Was that peace, and the order it implied, to be one of consent or one of coercion, one that safeguarded the right of self-determination or one that destroyed this right, one that provided an environment favorable to the growth of free institutions or one that encouraged the spread of arbitrary and irresponsible power? The fundamental issue raised by Vietnam, the Johnson Administration insisted throughout, was the issue of world order, an issue that could not be separated from American security.

The equation of world order and American security marked the lengths to which the policy of containment had been carried by the mid-1960s. The operational meaning of the American objective of world order was largely synonymous with opposition to the expansion of communism. World order was, in practice, containment writ large. The insistence upon equating the larger purpose of world order with security reflected the awareness that security continued to provide the principal justification for employing force, and that the invocation of security interests remained indispensable in order to sanction the costs of war. It was in the failure to make this equation persuasive that we must find the principal cause of the domestic dissent which arose in the course of the war. Other factors clearly contributed to this dissent, but they were not comparable to the failure to equate security with purpose, whether in Vietnam or in Asia as a whole.

The Nixon Administration was careful to avoid the appearance of attempting to restore the view entertained by its predecessor. Though continuing the war, it did so ostensibly on other grounds. The liberal and moderate criticism of American foreign policy that developed in the course of the Vietnam conflict had as its common denominator the overextension of American power. The Nixon Administration accepted the criticism, insisting only that change should not be "unsettling" and should not place American credibility in question. It was the latter consideration that largely explained the determination with which the Nixon Administration sought to vindicate the American commitment in Vietnam. An undisguised defeat in Vietnam, Nixon insisted, would set off a deep and sustained public reaction against further involvement abroad, thus undermining the necessary support for maintaining even a more modest role in the world than we had played in the pre-Vietnam period. Even a more modest role required the public's continued confidence in American power and the will of the president to use this power effectively when challenged. The same imperatives of prestige and credibility, this argument ran, held true for adversaries and allies, all the more so in a period marked by the modest retreat of American power. If the integrity of the larger structure of American interests was to be preserved, it was essential that this retreat not be undertaken, and not appear to be undertaken, as a response to defeat in Vietnam.

Thus the grounds on which the Nixon Administration continued the war in Vietnam were not the same as the grounds on which the preceding administration had taken up the conflict. Although refusing to endorse the principal critique brought against the war by liberal and moderate opponents, the rhetoric of the Nixon Administration appeared to accept much of the general thrust of this critique, a critique that—it is useful to recall—denied that there were any meaningful security interests at stake in Vietnam. Clearly, it was argued, this was true of the interests for which the war was allegedly undertaken in the first instance. Yet it was also held to be no less true of the interests for which the war was continued after victory had been all but openly abandoned. Vietnam had neither intrinsic nor symbolic importance for

American security. Even when judged from the perspective of the containment of China, its outcome was deemed largely irrelevant to the nation's legitimate security concerns. Instead, what Vietnam showed in the view of most critics were the absurd lengths to which a security rationale might be employed in circumstances that bore little relationship to those in which this rationale had once been meaningful and persuasive. In this liberal and moderate critique, Vietnam was above all the product of intellectual error.

The theme of intellectual error has found many expressions. In some sense this explanation is surely right, since we may assume that American leaders would have refrained from intervening in Vietnam (at least on such a massive scale) had they been able to foresee all the consequences of their actions. If intellectual error — a failure of political intelligence — is understood to mean no more than an inability to calculate the consequences of action, however roughly, then Vietnam must qualify as just that. Leslie Gelb apparently rejects even this meaning of intellectual error by his insistence that American involvement in Vietnam "did not stem from a failure to foresee consequences."* Yet his rejection is not consistently carried through, since he acknowledges that American policymakers hoped and believed that a strategy of escalation

---

*"Vietnam: The System Worked," *Foreign Policy* 3 (Summer 1971), p. 140. Also see Leslie H. Gelb with Richard K. Betts, *The Irony of Vietnam: The System Worked* (Washington, D.C.: Brookings Institution, 1979).

would eventually cause the communists to relent. Nor is it correct to say that the Johnson Administration's emphasis on Vietnam's "vitalness" was the result of intellectual default (though it may have been misleading). To argue, as Gelb and others have, that the issue of interest went unexamined is to apply a standard of interest — namely, a conventional security interest — that was evidently not the standard applied by those who deemed the intervention necessary. To argue that the Johnson Administration's emphasis on Vietnam's significance was mistaken is only to say that the war eventually threatened the larger interest it was intended to serve: the maintenance under American leadership of a stable world order that would insure the triumph of liberal-capitalist values and institutions. It was this larger interest — identified above as the interest in world order — that must ultimately explain Vietnam.

In the prevailing critique of the war, Vietnam resulted from a failure to understand the changes that had occurred over a generation and more, changes that had irrevocably altered while radically improving the American security position. So tenuous did the security arguments advanced on behalf of the war finally appear, and so solid did the rejection of these arguments seem, that it is not surprising that what was no more than a temporary constellation of forces was instead viewed at the time and in the immediate years to follow as virtually a permanent condition. The point has been made endlessly that the experience in Vietnam contributed more than any other event to the conviction that military power is of markedly declining utility in the contemporary world, particularly when employed in circumstances roughly comparable to those in Vietnam. This is certainly true, but the prolonged debate that attended the war also led to the belief that the world that had emerged by the middle to late 1960s, though far more complicated than the world of a generation earlier, was a much safer one. It was presumably a much safer world largely because it had become a far more pluralistic one. Interpreted, in essence, as the triumph of nationalism, pluralism was thought to mean that communist expansion was no longer the threat to America it had once been. Pluralism also meant that the prospect of Soviet expansion had dramatically declined. A pluralistic world pointed to a more disorderly world. But in the circumstances of the late 1960s and early 1970s this seemed a reasonable price to pay if such a world also pointed to a marked decline in the need for military intervention as a means for preserving vital American interests.

The debate engendered by Vietnam, it is important to recall, was not primarily a debate over America's vital interests in the world. Between defenders and conventional critics of the war, there was no marked difference in the definition of vital American interests. This was true even with respect to the Third World, where both sides agreed we had a vital interest in promoting and defending a certain kind of development. Liberal and moderate opposition to the war stemmed instead from the belief that the war could not have a successful outcome and that, whatever the outcome, the costs of war had become disproportionate to the interests at stake. It was particularly the latter argument that was stressed. Clearly, the weight of the argument depended upon the estimate made of the threat to American interests in Asia and elsewhere that would arise from failure in Vietnam. On this, liberal and moderate critics — in marked contrast to the minority of radical critics — were emphatic in discounting the threat to interests that might follow from defeat. This view reflected the more general estimate of their perception of the threat — or rather the lack thereof — to American interests posed by a world that was seen as inexorably moving toward greater and greater pluralism.

Yet it was not so much the optimistic expectations generally entertained of an increasingly pluralistic world that appear so striking in retrospect as it was the change that many, this writer included, found to have already occurred in the structure of American security.* Taken

---

*Robert W. Tucker, *Nation or Empire? The Debate Over American Foreign Policy* (Baltimore: Johns Hopkins University Press, 1968), p. 32. Surveying the changes that had occurred over a generation in the structure of American security, I concluded: "There is, in fact, no meaningful comparison to be drawn between the security position of this nation in the late nineteen-forties and its security position today. Whereas in the nineteen-forties it was still entirely possible, if not entirely plausible, to imagine an imbalance of military power that would threaten the physical security of America, today this contingency is no longer a meaningful possibility. Whereas in the nineteen-forties it was still entirely possible, and altogether plausible, to imagine an imbalance of power resulting in a security problem the solution of which would severely strain the nation's resources and jeopardize its democratic institutions, today this contingency is, at best, very remote."

alone, the appeal to pluralism as a refutation of the security rationale that led to Vietnam seemed, at best, inconclusive, but the argument that concentrated on the change in the structure of American security that had presumably occurred between the late 1940s and a generation later was another matter. It rested on what were the tried and true calculations that have always conditioned a nation's security—or so it seemed. On these calculations it no longer appeared plausible, let alone persuasive, to entertain the prospect of an imbalance of power resulting in a serious threat to our physical security, our economic well-being, or the integrity of our democratic institutions.

This estimate of the American security position reflected the circumstances of the middle to late 1960s and what were seen to be the changes contributing to the striking improvement in that position. Although the mood at the turn of the preceding decade had been markedly pessimistic, it had clearly altered by the time we became fully committed in Vietnam. The events of the early 1960s, and above all the Cuban missile crisis, had dissipated earlier fears that the tides of world politics were turning against the United States. Whereas in the late 1950s the conditions of competition between America and the communist nations were widely seen as favoring a communism still regarded as monolithic, by the mid-1960s these conditions were seen as having been dramatically reversed. In the period following the Cuban missile crisis, not only did the United States emerge in a position of marked military and economic preponderance, but it did so at a time when the last semblance of any pretense to unity between the major communist powers was dropped and intense rivalry was openly acknowledged. Even the prospects in the developing world appeared to have changed. A few years before, the Soviets and Chinese were considered to enjoy most of the advantages in the competition for influence and position in the Third World; now the judgment was reversed and conditions marking the "crucial transitional process" were considered to favor an outcome congenial to American interests.

It was in these circumstances that the contest with the Soviet Union began to abate. Yet it was also in these circumstances that America undertook the war in Vietnam. Despite the Johnson Administration's rationale for the intervention, the war was not entered into in the despairing expectation of a world balance of power that was turning against us. Instead, it was begun and, until a later stage, prosecuted under the confident assumption of "America preponderant." Ironically, most critics of the war largely shared this assumption. Where they did not, they could still believe in the benign effects of an ever stronger pluralism.

A wiser counsel would have cautioned — as a few did caution — that no power constellation is guaranteed to endure, that the persistence of a favorable power balance cannot be taken for granted, and that this particular constellation of power, like so many such constellations in the past, might also prove to be fragile and mutable. We can now see only too clearly that the foundations on which this constellation rested were beginning to erode even at the time that their solidity was being so confidently proclaimed. The degree of security it appeared to afford depended on a favorable balance of military power that could be maintained, if at all, only by measures that were not taken.

Instead, the policy adopted by the Johnson Administration, and subsequently given formal expression by the Nixon Administration, accepted the Soviet Union as the equal—or soon to be equal—of this country in strategic military power. How this policy might be safely reconciled with the continued integrity of American vital interests and commitments in Europe, the Middle East, and Asia, particularly if the United States together with its allies did not enjoy parity in conventional military power with the Soviet Union, was never satisfactorily explained.

In retrospect, Kissinger, a principal steward of this policy, has provided the most acute criticism of it:

> . . . the change in the strategic situation produced by our limited vulnerability is more fundamental for the United States than even total vulnerability would be for the Soviet Union because our strategic doctrine has relied extraordinarily, perhaps exclusively, on our superior strategic power. The Soviet Union has never relied on its superior strategic power. It has always depended more on its local

50

and regional superiority. Therefore, even an equivalence in destructive power, even "assured destruction" for both sides, is a revolution in the strategic balance as we have known it.*

Kissinger also notes that one reason for the "amazing phenomenon which historians will ponder" — that is, the failure of the United States to make a significant effort to rectify the state of affairs resulting from the massive growth of Soviet strategic forces — was the growth of a school of thought "which considered that strategic stability was a military asset, and in which the historically amazing theory developed that vulnerability contributed to peace and invulnerability contributed to risks of war."

At that time there were, of course, explanations, even ingenious ones. But these explanations never persuasively addressed the central issue of what would effectively restrain the Soviet Union from taking such advantage as it safely could of an ever improving military position. Instead, they largely proceeded from the undemonstrated assumption that the Soviet Union had become — or was in the process of becoming — a status quo power. As such, it could now be expected to act with growing restraint.

---

*Opening remarks to a NATO conference, held in Brussels, September 1–3, 1979. Reprinted as "The Future of NATO," in Henry Kissinger, *For the Record: Selected Statements 1977–1980* (Boston: Little, Brown, 1981), p. 239.

When in the face of evidence to the contrary, this assumption began to wear thin, many fell back on the argument that even if the Soviet Union was intent upon expanding its influence and would employ its growing military power to this end, the forces of resistance thrown up by a determinedly pluralistic world would ultimately frustrate its efforts.

Applied to areas of secondary interest, which also happen to be areas that are not contiguous to the Soviet Union, the merit of this argument may not prove to be of crucial concern. When applied to areas of primary interest that are also adjacent to the Soviet Union, or very nearly so, it is. With respect to these areas, among which the Persian Gulf is the prime case, the reliance on pluralism was and is little more than an expression of hope.

The degree of security that only yesterday was taken for granted also rested on the assumption that continued Western access to the raw materials — above all, energy — of the developing world could be assured on terms compatible with substantial economic growth of the industrial democracies. Ironically, Vietnam and the debate it precipitated appeared to many to confirm this assumption. America had entered the war, it was held, largely out of an excessive preoccupation in the 1960s with the Third World. Instead, the prevailing argument ran, the emergence of a pluralistic world meant that the significance previously given the developing countries could be downgraded. We were not in Vietnam, as a minority of radical critics of the war contended, because the greater stake in the conflict was continued access to indispensable raw materials on Western terms, but because we had misunderstood the changes that had taken place in the world, and above all in the developing countries. An eminent commentator articulated the new understanding in noting that by any power calculus the states of the Third World

> have no vital relation to the economic or strategic position of the developed countries. They do supply raw materials. But even here the typical observation concerns not their power as sources of such supply, but rather their weakness as competitive hewers of wood in the markets of the industrially advanced countries.*

These words were written when the storm was already gathering. In respect to one transcendentally important raw material, oil, demand was already pressing hard on supply. Rather than opting to increase supply, and to remain competitive "hewers of wood," the producers chose to combine and to impose a fourfold increase in the price of their oil. At the time of the increase, some producers also initiated a limited embargo against states whose policies in the 1973 Arab-Israeli war were considered objectionable. Neither of these measures provoked

---

*John Kenneth Galbraith, "Plain Lessons of a Bad Decade," *Foreign Policy* (Winter 1970–71), p. 37.

significant Western reaction. Both challenged the foundations of the postwar order as no other event had since the 1940s.

Quite apart from the constraints on economic growth that OPEC policy placed on the industrial democracies, the failure in 1973–74 to respond to the Arab oil embargo raised from the outset the issue of right of access to the oil supplies of the Persian Gulf. Obscured for a time by the preoccupation with the economic side of the crisis, the issue of access became apparent with the Iranian revolution, which shut off most of the production of a major producer. In swift succession, the Soviet invasion of Afghanistan revealed the potential external threat to Western access, while the outbreak of war between Iraq and Iran illuminated yet another aspect of the indigenous threat to what remains of the Western position.

3

It is in the coalescence of these two momentous developments—a military balance increasingly favorable to the Soviet Union and the steady erosion of Western power and position in the Persian Gulf—that the essential dimensions of the American security problem are to be seen today. The point has often been made that in its origins and subsequent course, the energy crisis had very little to do with the Soviet Union. Indeed, the Soviets have been—at least until recently—quite cautious and tentative in taking such advantage as they might have from the decline of the Western position in the Gulf.

Though on balance this point is well taken, at present it is not possible to separate the issue of Western access to the Gulf from the military power the Soviet Union is able to bring to bear in order to inhibit and, it may be, to openly challenge the attempted reassertion of Western power in this vital region.

In the light of these considerations, if we are to judge the significance of the present debate over foreign policy by way of comparison with the past, it is to the late 1940s that we must look and not the late 1960s. The prospect that was virtually dismissed by most observers only a short time ago has materialized again. The fear that was entertained at the outset of the cold war, that the Soviet Union might succeed in extending its sway over Western Europe, is once again entertained.

Nor is this fear any less plausible today than it was in an earlier period, and this despite the great changes that have since transpired. The military balance was no more favorable to the Soviet Union in the late 1940s than it is today. If anything, it was less favorable then, the still prostrate condition of Western Europe notwithstanding. For if the American strategic capability then was miniscule as compared with what it is today, it was still considerable, while the Soviet capability of striking directly at the United States was nonexistent. Were the worst to have come, Western Europe would have been the helpless prey of the Soviet Union. At the same time, Soviet industrial and population centers would have been the helpless prey of the strategic power of a still physically invulnerable America.

The objection will no doubt be made to this comparison that the military balance as such cannot usefully be considered in isolation from the other circumstances conditioning the security of nations. In the late 1940s Western Europe was not only still economically prostrate, but was also politically and psychologically vulnerable. It was this vulnerability that some saw at the time and continue to see in retrospect as the real threat held out to Western Europe, and not the threat of Soviet arms. Undoubtedly, the ravages of a brutal war, the shock of defeat, and the pervasive conviction that Europe was historically spent led to a profound crisis of self-confidence that found expression in an acute sense of vulnerability. Even so, an important part of Europe's sense of vulnerability could not be distinguished from the threat of Soviet arms. Nor, in fact, was it so separated by most Western Europeans.

In circumstances that in many respects are so radically changed, this sense of vulnerability has revived today. The oil crisis has accentuated it as perhaps no other factor, including the relentless buildup of Soviet arms. Were Western Europe to be denied the oil of the Persian Gulf, its economic life would come to a sudden halt.

The loss of physical access need not be equated with a literal cut off from the oil supplies of the Gulf. This is one possible consequence of losing access. It forms the extreme or limiting case, and although it may never come to pass, the possibility alone of its occurrence is sufficient to condition the behavior of those who have lost their former position but who remain as dependent as ever on the resources of the Gulf. In all likelihood, the West would continue to get something that roughly approximates its present share of Persian Gulf oil regardless of the power that controlled access to the oil. But it would get the oil only on the economic and political terms laid down by those who enjoyed control.

This is the situation we have been moving toward for some time with respect to the producing countries. Step by step, the major consumers in the West have surrendered such leverage as they once exercised over the producers. In turn, the latter have increasingly laid down the economic and political terms on which the former may receive oil. Walter Levy has recently written that "Because of the fear of being arbitrarily cut off from supplies, Western nations and their companies now accept within a wide range practically any economic or political terms that a producing country may impose on them."* Levy observes that this subservience has only encouraged producing countries to proceed as they see fit, which has meant in an increasingly arbitrary manner. He concludes that we have entered a period in international oil of near "lawlessness." But this is only to say that the major Western consumers have on almost every occasion backed away from the attempt to apply countervailing power against the producing countries. In this manner, they

---

*Walter J. Levy, "Oil and the Decline of the West," *Foreign Affairs* (Summer 1980), p. 1004.

have gone very far toward surrendering physical access in its most elemental sense.

Whether this situation, one without real parallel in the history of state relations, might have persisted in the absence of the Soviet Union must remain an open question. It does not seem plausible to assume that it could, for that assumption requires us to believe that the nations of the West, though incomparably more powerful than the principal Middle East oil producing countries, would go on indefinitely in their acceptance of actions that jeopardize their economic and, ultimately, political well-being. It requires us to believe that despite the prospect of chronic bouts of inflation and recession, that despite the recurrent threat to the international financial system, the Western countries would continue to remain supine before the demands of the major producers, with the result that wealth and power would pass in ever increasing measure from the hands of those who only yesterday could scarcely have imagined their plight of today.

Given the record of Western behavior in the past decade, it must be conceded that the above assumption cannot be simply dismissed. From the emergence of Khaddafi to the advent of Khomeini, this record is one that will surely fascinate, while mystifying, future historians. Never before have power and position been given up with such alacrity and in circumstances that plainly did not require their abandonment. Never before have nations that possessed so great a superiority in power as the Western countries possessed over the Middle East producers placed themselves in so needless and so dangerous a predicament. At any one of a number of points, the dangerous slide might have been arrested and even reversed. Until that slide was well advanced, it had little if anything to do with the Soviet Union. On the contrary, what is surprising, as Elie Kedourie has noted, "is that so much time should have elapsed between the visible erosion of Western power and prestige in the Middle East and the inescapable conclusions the Soviet Union was bound to draw from this willfully self-destructive conduct."* Though the Soviets may now be expected to take such advantage as they can of the Western descent from grace — why should they not? — it was not the Soviets who initiated the descent and gave it the momentum it soon acquired.

These considerations notwithstanding, it strains credulity to assume that the process we have witnessed could have continued indefinitely in the absence of the Soviet Union. Sooner or later, the consequences of continuing on the course followed since the late 1960s would almost certainly have led to a reaction in the countries of the West and to the reassertion of a control that has been so readily relinquished. Governments that refused to take the measures necessary for such reassertion would have been replaced by governments that accepted the need for

---

*Elie Kedourie, "Western Deference in the Mideast," *New Republic* (June 7, 1980), p. 19.

taking them. There are, after all, limits to the thralldom in which a political pathology may hold those who have not lost all sense of reality. In the past year or two we have begun to press against those limits. The consequences of the sudden deprivation of Iranian production, the leap in prices, the increasing subservience demanded by the producing states, and above all the growing realization that all this might well be only the harbinger of greater things to come were beginning at long last to have their effects. Without the dramatic demonstration of Soviet power, they might well have issued in the attempt to redress the balance between producers and consumers and, more particularly, to reassert a measure of Western control over the Persian Gulf.

Now as in the past, the states of the Gulf cannot literally defend themselves against a substantial outside force from either the Soviet Union or the West. All they can do is attempt to deter such outside forces from being used by threatening to blow up the oil fields in response to military intervention. This threat has been voiced with varying ambiguity for some five years, particularly by Saudi officials. In the West, it has been taken with the utmost seriousness. Indeed, many expert observers consider the destruction of the oil facilities a virtual certainty in the event of outside intervention, though why they should do so is by no means apparent. Destruction of the oil fields cannot serve a defensive purpose, as does a scorched earth policy, for it will not make the invader's conduct of military operations more difficult. Even if the destruction is thorough, it denies the invader his objective only for a limited period. The threat of such denial as a deterrent may make sense depending upon the time required for repairing the destruction and the state of need of the invader. The same threat as a defense makes very little sense.

As a deterrent, the threat to destroy the oil fields may have only limited effect on those who have no desperate need for continuous oil supplies. This consideration is relevant not only to the Soviet Union but also to such obvious local disturbers of the fragile peace of the Gulf as Iraq. If the limited number and fragility of the ports and pump sites that control the flow of oil from the Gulf are such that any outside military intervention would result in their almost certain destruction, the same result must be held as likely to follow from any serious outbreak of conflict involving only the local states. If there were any doubt of this before the Iraqis and the Iranians began bombing each other's oil installations in Fall 1980, there can be no doubt of it now. To argue that the oil installations of the Gulf can only be put to the torch by outside incendiarists may serve the purposes of those who are at pains to counsel against the threat of military intervention by the West, but it cannot relieve us of the prospect that a sustained interruption in the oil supplies of the Gulf might well result despite our prudence — or, rather, our passivity.

Given the very considerable potential for further turbulence in the region, the prospects for enjoying continuous oil supplies in the years ahead must be rated as quite low. Once this is accepted, then at least one of the great objections to any attempt by the West to reassert its power in the Gulf must be largely discarded. The Soviet reaction apart, little would be jeopardized by such reassertion that irrespective of our wishes would not be jeopardized through other developments; and a great deal might be gained.

These considerations have been obscured only because there has long been a near universal determination in the West not to acknowledge the stark alternatives that confront us in the Persian Gulf. Although it is admitted that some power(s) must control the region, the pretense is maintained that the power(s) may be the local states and this despite their weakness relative to outside powers and their marked instability. This pretense requires us to believe that the key to global power for another generation will remain in the hands of those who, even when taken collectively, represent a virtual power vacuum.

Time will surely lay bare this illusion for what it is. The vital resource of the Gulf can no more remain independent of superpower control than Europe in 1945 could remain outside the effective sphere of both Soviet and American power. In retrospect, it is possible to imagine at least one of the superpowers having extended its sway over the whole of Europe. It is much easier to imagine that the line of division could have been drawn other than where it was. But it is scarcely possible to conceive of the continent that had once been the center of the international system, and that had been suddenly transformed into a power vacuum through war and defeat, not attracting a competition for control by the two great victors. In defeat, Europe still represented the vital stake for the newly emergent superpowers that had displaced it. The conflict that quickly arose over control of the continent was, given its structural causes, as predictable as anything can be in politics. Only the outcome was indeterminate.

In one sense at least, and it is all important, the parallel that may be drawn between Europe in the 1940s and the Persian Gulf today is apparent and striking. Almost as certainly as did Europe in the 1940s, the Gulf provides *the* critical source of conflict between the United States and the Soviet Union. What in Europe resulted from war and defeat, in the Middle East has resulted from the withdrawal of the power (Great Britain) that once controlled the region and the subsequent refusal of the United States to fill the vacuum. In an area that was as significant for American interests in the 1970s as Europe was in the 1940s, the attempt was instead made to find local substitutes for the power this country refused to commit, whether in the form of a regional surrogate (Iran) or in the form of a progressive settlement of the Arab-Israeli conflict that would presumably satisfy the Arab states and leave them indebted to, and aligned with, this country. A policy that appeared more ambitious than ever when measured by the scope of its aims and the degree of its involvement was in fact rooted in a declining power position relative to both the Soviet Union and the states of the region. Indeed, the very ambitiousness of American policy, particularly when measured by the attempt to exclude the Soviet Union from playing a significant role in the region, reflected — paradoxically enough — a sense of growing vulnerability rather than of growing strength. Obscured for a time, the results of this policy have now been fully exposed.

Whatever the outcome of the crisis in the Persian Gulf, it seems reasonably clear that the present situation is unlikely to persist for long. This is so not because of its economic implications, grave as they undoubtedly are and will continue to be, but because of its strategic implications. The vacuum that the Gulf represents today will be filled. Since it cannot be filled by local power that does not exist and cannot be suddenly materialized by political incantation, it will be filled by outside power.

This can only mean that it will be controlled by either the United States, the Soviet Union, or a condominium of the two. There remains the outside chance that none of these prospects will materialize because of the fear each superpower may entertain of the reaction of the other should it move to fill the vacuum. In this event the vacuum in the Gulf would persist and Western interests would remain vulnerable to developments resulting in the denial of access to the oil supplies of the Gulf. The net effect of the perpetuation of the present situation would clearly be of advantage to the Soviet Union, and for this reason it represents an outcome the Soviets would favor should the proper conditions for an optimal outcome not materialize. Still, the very importance of the Gulf, when taken together with its pervasive instability, make this prospect a highly unlikely one.

This being so, we are required to consider the alternatives. If the Gulf is eventually controlled, whether directly or indirectly by the Soviet Union, the post–World War II political structure will suffer sudden destruction. The loss of the Gulf could be expected to form an almost certain prelude to the effective end of the American position in Western Europe and Japan. Dependent as they would then be on the Soviet Union for oil, these nations would adjust their policies and actions to Moscow's wishes. Even if the Soviet Union did not immediately insist that they break their security ties with the United States, these ties would be deprived of any substantive meaning. In these circumstances, no real purpose would be served by the retention of an American security presence in Europe, even if this presence were not asked to leave. In the 1940s the Soviet Union could threaten Western Europe's physical security only if it was prepared to endure American reprisals to which it could not directly respond. Today the Soviet Union, once in control of the Persian Gulf, could dispose of Western Europe's economic life. A militarily superior position in Europe would serve to reinforce a control that the United States would be powerless to contest.

4

What is significant about the present debate over American foreign policy is its unexpected familiarity. At issue are essentially the same security interests that were at issue in the years immediately following World War II. If the locus of the now most likely threat to those interests has shifted from Europe to the Persian Gulf, the vital interests at stake in the Gulf remain unchanged from the vital interests that were earlier at stake in Europe. This is not seriously questioned by any of the participants in the present debate, for no one argues that the loss of Western access to the Gulf could eventuate in anything short of a mortal blow to the post–World War II structure of America's global interests. No one argues that such a loss to the Soviet Union could have any other result. What is disputed is the Soviet intention to challenge Western access. This dispute is not unlike the dispute that arose in the 1940s over Moscow's intentions toward Europe. Short of the materialization of intention through action the present controversy is likely to prove as inconclusive as its predecessor.

Yet the consequences of Soviet control of the Persian Gulf cannot be shunted aside by speculation on Soviet intentions. Even if those intentions were more benign than we could have plausible reason for assuming, the structural causes of conflict over control of the Gulf would remain. They can no more be spirited away than could the causes that led to conflict after World War II.

Quite apart from the structural causes of conflict over the Gulf, why should the Soviets not aspire to extend their control over this vital area? Even if the Soviet state were something quite different from what it is, the aspiration to achieve a position of global preponderance would operate with a magnetic pull on Moscow's rulers, particularly if their military position were as strong as the Soviet Union's is today. That we are not dealing with "another Russia" but with the Communist Russia of today makes the consequences of the ensuing struggle over the Persian Gulf far more serious.

The parallel thus apparent between the immediate postwar years and today is striking. Like any parallel, it can be pushed too far. The differences in the circumstances attending Western Europe in the late 1940s and the Persian Gulf today are also striking. Whereas Western Europe was relatively stable, despite appearances to the contrary, the Persian Gulf is a nightmare of real and potential instability. Whereas Western Europe on balance welcomed the American "intervention," the states of the Persian Gulf are still very far from doing so. It is the latter difference that has received considerable emphasis and that vitiates, in the judgment of many observers, if not the parallel drawn here then at least the prospect that a comparable response to that made in an earlier period is possible today. In this judgment the states of the region hold it within their power to deny Western access and to defeat any attempt to force them to grant access to their oil supplies.

But this judgment is almost certainly misplaced. If, contrary to all reasonable expectations, the power vacuum in the Persian Gulf does persist, its very persistence would herald a transformation of revolutionary proportion in the international system. The outcome would confirm what has now been contended for more than a decade: that certain traditional forms of power, especially military power, have now been substantially deprived of their former utility.

Were this contention to be borne out by events, the Western predicament in the Persian Gulf would very likely issue in the altogether grim prospects that have been recently outlined by Walter Levy.* Rather than the Soviet Union, the great threat to the stability and security of the West would come from the very vacuum that the West must continue to rely upon but cannot effectively fill. In these circumstances, the military power of the Soviet Union would presumably prove as impotent as that of the West. But in these circumstances as well, the military power of the Soviet Union could in general be safely neglected. What this power could not do in the Persian Gulf, it also could not be expected to do in Western Europe.

---

*Walter J. Levy, "Oil and the Decline of the West," *Foreign Affairs* (Summer 1980), pp. 999–1015.

IV

The Arms Balance and the Persian Gulf

1

If we assume the persistence of a more traditional world, we have little alternative but to respond to a conventional security threat in the way that states have regularly responded to such threats. An imbalance of military power, present or prospective, must be met by counter-vailing military power. We have no choice when faced by threats that, if permitted to go unmet, could result in sacrificing interests on which the nation's economic well-being and the integrity of its basic institutions depend. The purist may cavil even at this restricted meaning given to necessity in foreign policy, but short of circumstances in which an insoluble conflict between physical security and the other attributes commonly identified with security is demonstrably apparent, it will suffice.

The case for considering our immediate options today as very narrow is difficult to contest. Admittedly, it is still contested, as the continuing debate over America's proper policy in the Persian Gulf testifies. Even so, the shifting nature of that debate also demonstrates the compelling force of vital interest once a threat to it becomes inescapably clear. Confronted with the stark alternatives of risking loss of access to the oil supplies of the Gulf, or of deploying military power to prevent such a loss, the Carter Administration had no choice in the end but to respond to a vital interest.

Its response was marked by ambiguity. In implementation, it was faltering and tortuous. But whatever criticism one may make of it, there was a response. Moreover, under the impact of events that have left little room for doubt over the straitened position of the West in the Persian Gulf, this response gathered momentum. A comparison of the American position in the region in Fall 1979 with the nation's position in late Fall 1980 reveals the extent of the change that has taken place, a change that was clearly uncongenial to President Carter and that he resisted until events left him no meaningful choice.

More generally, the compelling force of vital interest has left us no meaningful choice in deciding whether or not we will respond to the continuing arms buildup of the Soviet Union with an improved military position of our own. The manner and emphasis, the pace and magnitude of the response continue to elicit controversy. The diplomatic consequences that some fear rearmament to hold out provoke even greater controversy. These and still other considerations notwithstanding, a majority among elites and public alike now accepts the imminent prospect—if not the present reality—of an overall arms balance that favors the Soviet Union. The need to redress this actual or prospective imbalance is also broadly accepted.

The wellspring of this consensus must be traced to the growing conviction that the United States has steadily moved throughout the past decade toward an insolvent foreign policy. This is true whether in the Persian Gulf—where commitment was not in accord with interest and where the means to sustain interest or commitment were almost totally lacking—or in Western Europe—where credibility of commitment was increasingly called into question by the growing inadequacy of the necessary means. The remedy for a foreign policy that has come close to insolvency because the means to secure vital interests are inadequate is plainly to restore the necessary means. In the two most critical areas of concern to the United States, the necessary means—not the only means but the necessary means—are military. This point deserves particular emphasis with respect to the Persian Gulf. Though it is here that the need is greatest, it is also here that the temptation persists to find a substitute for this need.

The experience of a decade, however, has amply demonstrated the truth that should have been apparent from the outset: there is no reliable substitute for

Western power in the Gulf. The continued search for such a substitute — whether in the form of another American surrogate, of alignment with the West by means of a regional arrangement, or of collective nonalignment — is entirely vain. The conditions of domestic instability and of intraregional rivalries that characterize the Gulf render any and all of these schemes either impossible to achieve or without real value even if apparently achieved.

Nor is there any plausible reason for believing that these schemes would prove feasible and effective if a satisfactory settlement of the Palestinian issue were achieved. A settlement of the Palestinian issue would not materially lessen the need for Western power in the Gulf because it would not remove the many sources of conflict and instability in the region. Of the major events that have shaken the Gulf in the past two years and that have threatened Western access — notably the fall of the Shah and the Iraqi-Iranian war — none has had more than a peripheral relationship to the Palestinian issue. The continued insistence upon seeing in a comprehensive settlement of the Arab-Israeli conflict a critical part — indeed, *the* critical part — of the solution to Western vulnerability in the Gulf has become the refuge of those who do not believe there can be an effective reassertion of Western power and that, this being so, we must clutch at such straws as best we can.

A recent variation on this view holds that Arab states of the Gulf — particularly Saudi Arabia — would be more receptive to an American military presence if the Pales-

tinian issue were to be satisfactorily resolved.* Those urging this view seem oblivious to the notorious fact that
there is no consensus among Arab states on what a "satisfactory" solution would consist of and that such a consensus is not likely to emerge. The argument that the recep-
tivity of the Gulf states to an American presence depends
on the politics of the area is surely right. But it does not
follow that the Palestinian issue is the key to a favorable
attitude of the Gulf states toward a Western military
presence on their territory. Instead, the key is a restoration of American credibility, a restoration that will not be
furthered by an America that is seen to be pressuring
Israel on the Palestinian issue *in order to* improve its
standing in the Arab world. If anything, such pressure is
likely to have the opposite effect from those its advocates
claim it would have. The Saudis will see it not as an indication of American credibility but as further evidence
of the weakness of our position.

A comprehensive settlement of the Arab-Israeli conflict—assuming, for the sake of argument, that this is
possible within the foreseeable future—would prove
largely unresponsive to the dangers we face in the Gulf.
No conceivable settlement of the Palestinian issue would
materially affect the aspirations of Iraq, the continuing
storm in Iran, or the deeper causes of instability in Saudi

---

*See David Watt, "The Atlantic Alliance Needs Leaders Who Face the
Facts," *Economist,* October 11, 1980, p. 26.

Arabia. Nor would it deter the Soviets from taking such action as they might take in the absence of a settlement.

From the outset of the search for a comprehensive settlement, the reasoning of those intent on obtaining it has been that without such settlement or visible progress toward achieving it, another round of conflict in the near future is inevitable. Another round of conflict, this reasoning goes, promises a repetition of the events attending the 1973 war, only this time with results that may prove disastrous. But as the Iraqi-Iranian war has once again demonstrated, the contingencies that are so feared —interruption of the flow of oil and confrontation with the Soviet Union—may still arise in the absence of another round of conflict between Israel and its protagonists. Any number of events might lead to at least a partial cutting off of oil supplies. Any number of events might also bring an extension of Soviet influence or control in the Gulf. On the other hand, so long as the peace between Egypt and Israel holds, one of the least likely prospects is another Arab-Israeli war because it would be foolhardy for Israel's remaining adversaries to initiate war without Egypt.

If Washington and its Western European allies are intent on avoiding another Arab-Israeli war, they should be doing all that is within their power to consolidate the peace achieved at Camp David. An obsession with the Palestinian problem will risk doing the opposite. If the Western states are willing to do for the PLO and their supporters what they are unable to do for themselves, there will be little incentive for serious negotiations.

More serious still, if the West places supreme importance upon achieving what it deems to be the rights of the Palestinians, Sadat can scarcely afford to take the position of demanding less. A renewed drive for a comprehensive settlement endangers the partial settlement that must still be consolidated.

2

These considerations seem so apparent that one is driven to ask why at this late date they nevertheless remain so widely resisted. What betokens, Elie Kedourie asks,

> a restless and dangerous quest for schemes and combinations which, soberly considered, are both shaky and profitless: to satisfy the PLO is to satisfy the Arabs, to satisfy the Arabs is to have them on our side, to have them on our side is . . . what? To compel the evacuation of Afghanistan? To deter the Soviets? To secure the price of oil? At prices which do not irresistibly go up?*

The questions are no more than rhetorical. Kedourie rightly concludes that

> The real reason for all these agitations is the profound reluctance of Western powers to do what is required in order to protect their own interests: namely, to make their strength visible and respected. Only they can reestablish the balance which past illusions and fecklessness allowed to be upset.

---

*Kedourie, "Western Deference in the Mideast," p. 21.

Unfortunately, the illusions and fecklessness of which Kedourie speaks continue to find expression, as the Vance speech at Harvard and the favorable reception accorded that speech testify.* Stanley Hoffmann finds the former secretary's pronouncement an "admirable" antidote to those who fail to appreciate that, in Vance's words, "increased military power is a basis, not a substitute, for diplomacy," and who believe "that America could have the power to order the world just the way we want it to be."† Given the power disposed of by the Soviet Union, Hoffman warns, "these are the hallmarks of global calamity." And so, indeed, they are, as every sensible person would agree. They are as unexceptionable as the admonitions that diplomacy cannot be effective without adequate military power and that America is not wholly impotent in its ability to affect world order—and about as instructive.

The purpose of the Vance speech, however, was not to give the nation an introductory lesson in the conduct of foreign policy. It was to register opposition to the shift in administration policy that began in Fall 1979 and, even more, to warn against any further hardening of policy. With respect to the Persian Gulf, the Carter Doctrine must have represented the limits of Vance's endurance, else why his emphasis—otherwise certainly out of place when directed to the Carter Administration—on the

---

*New York Times, June 6, 1980, p. A12.

†Stanley Hoffmann, "The Crisis in the West," New York Review of Books (July 17, 1980), pp. 41ff.

"dangerous fallacy of the military solution to nonmilitary problems" and his warning that "the use of military force is not, and should not be, a desirable American policy response to the internal politics of other nations"?

Hoffmann has filled in the gaps left by Vance. In the guise of presenting the "average Western European view" — which is, in effect his view as well — Hoffmann finds the Carter Doctrine "militaristic and simplistic." It demands that the states of the Gulf choose between East and West, thus ruling out a position of nonalignment that "constitutes the best obstacle to Soviet advances." From a yet broader perspective, the American approach is seen as neglecting "all the factors and forces, other than the military balance, that explain the predicament of the United States in the Persian Gulf and can be neither suppressed nor superseded by force alone, such as the Arab-Israeli conflict, or the internal weaknesses of the Saudi regime, or the Iranian internal turmoil." It is presumably these factors more than the absence of substantial and effectively deployed and deployable military forces in the Gulf that impair the Western position and endanger Western interests.

The significance of this criticism cannot be appreciated by taking it at face value, for at face value it makes very little sense. How will collective nonalignment do what alignment cannot do? Certainly, it cannot somehow confer on the nonaligned a strength they otherwise do not have. It may be argued that nonalignment would not provide a source of internal division that a policy of alignment would provide, and that it would not, for this reason, afford the Soviets with a justification for direct or indirect intervention. Even if the argument is accepted, it does not follow that nonalignment holds out a reasonable promise of deterring Soviet advances. Nonaligned, the states of the region will still remain weak, they will still be ridden with instabilities, and they will still present the Soviet Union with numerous opportunities to exploit these instabilities.

The charge that the American approach neglects all factors and forces other than military balance is very nearly the opposite of the truth, both in the past and at present. What has been neglected is precisely the military balance. This is the major reason we find ourselves in the precarious position we do today. But suppose we were to direct greater attention and effort to these other factors and forces. Apart from the Arab-Israeli conflict, could we have more than a marginal effect on their outcomes? If these factors and forces really explain the American predicament in the Gulf, then we had best conclude that our predicatment is hopeless because it is certain that they will persist, and probably worsen, in the years ahead.

Is this Hoffmann's conclusion? He will not admit to it. What first needs to be done, he argues, is to counter the influence of those who are obsessed with military power, who see in it a substitute for diplomacy, and who long to return to a *Pax Americana.* Confronted with the Soviet invasion of Afghanistan and with what Hoffman concedes to be the "enormous military advantage" the USSR enjoys in the Persian Gulf region, his "first imperative" of action is to declare war against the domestic adversary, those who trade in "oversimplifying and hysterical interpretations of Soviet behavior" and who find the Soviets as "ten feet tall, as manipulaing countless forces in countless countries, as devilishly clever, scheming, and successful, and *also* assert that a simple overwhelming display of military might would drive all our troubles away." Presumably, once the truly dangerous domestic adversary is silenced, the "enormous military advantages" the USSR enjoys may be seen in their proper perspective.

This proper perspective is revealed by understanding Soviet interests and goals. "Any serious analysis of Soviet policies and statements," we are informed, reveals a "profound insecurity," a pervasive ambition to be "recognized as an equal superpower and accepted by the U.S. as a co-manager of world affairs, with equal rights and equal say," and a willingness to oblige Washington to treat Moscow as an equal, if it does not do so voluntarily. Whether this is an adequate statement of what "any serious analysis of Soviet policies and statements reveals" need not detain us here. For our purposes, it may be accepted. The relevant question, then, is its bearing on our predicament in the Persian Gulf. If Moscow is insistent upon "equal rights and equal say," and willing to "oblige" Washington to treat it as an equal, what does this mean for the region on which the West and Japan are vitally dependent and where Moscow possesses "enormous military advantages"?

79

Hoffmann's answer is first to remind us that Soviet moves in Africa and around the Persian Gulf since 1975 are probably "in considerable part a response to our 'exclusion' of the Soviets from the Middle Eastern peace process." But even if we were to accept this view without question, what may be said to follow from it? Are we to conclude that if we were to reintroduce the Soviets into the peace process—thereby abandoning in effect Camp David—our predicament in the Gulf would be, if not resolved, materially eased? Hoffmann will not say so, and for good reason. He will not even clearly say that we should now admit the USSR as a partner into the peace process, jsut as he will not say that we should grant the Soviets "equal rights and equal say" in general and in the Persian Gulf in particular for the reason that "their regime violates our deepest beliefs, and its ambitions threaten our strategic, economic, and political positions."

Yet he counsels us to keep trying "to turn an adversary relationship into a mixed one" and to understand "that what is at stake is not an untenable status quo but the management of inevitable change." Only then "will the Soviet drive for status become less maniacal, more differentiated, and our resistance to it less fierce and more discriminating." Hoffmann's specific prescription for getting past the immediate crisis is to explore the possibility of a bargain whereby in exchange for Soviet commitment to withdraw its forces from Afghanistan and to accept an enlargement of the present Afghan regime, we would guarantee Afghanistan's neutrality, resume arms control negotiations on a comprehensive test ban, resubmit SALT II to the Senate, move toward a speedy SALT III negotiation, and link the Camp David process — now played out — to a renewed search for a comprehensive settlement (acknowledging at the outset of the "search" the "Palestinian right to self-determination").

What is all this but a sophisticated way of proposing that we move over in those areas from which we have heretofore sought to exclude the Soviets and thereby adjust — in large part, at least — to their interests? The "untenable status quo" the changing of which will lead to the moderation of Soviet policy is a status quo that has in the past favored Western, and particularly American, interests and that in the future must prove more favorable to Soviet interests. Otherwise there is no reason to expect that change will lead to an amelioration in Soviet policy. If this is indeed the meaning of Hoffman's advice, why not state it more directly and candidly? Why equivocate and even mislead on the issue of "equal rights and equal say"?

As for the "bargain" with the Soviet Union that Hoffmann suggests exploring, a Soviet withdrawal from Afghanistan cannot be secured by the promise of that country's "neutrality," for Moscow can have no confidence in a Kabul government it does not control, especially in the light of what has transpired in Afghanistan. A formula of neutralization must insure Moscow's control, in which case the term neutrality is merely a euphemism, or it is worthless. Yet if that is indeed the meaning of neutrality in the Afghan context, how is it a "bargain" in return for which we make the other concessions Hoffman proposes? Even if these objections are put aside, how would a "renewed search" for a comprehensive settlement of the Arab-Israeli conflict (again a euphemism since in "acknowledging the Palestinian right to self-determination" as a precondition, what is paraded as a search is in reality a settlement) alleviate, let alone resolve, our predicament in the Persian Gulf? Would the Soviets then abandon their aspirations in that region or be forced to do so because of the obstacle to their ambitions that would appear in the form of the imposing barrier of nonalignment?

At the root of Hoffmann's apparently complex analysis is something quite simple. He does not wish to redress the present imbalance of power in the only way that imbalances can be redressed, with countervailing power. At the same time he does not wish to acknowledge the possible (even likely) consequences of failing to redress the imbalance. Thus the resolution with which he turns on those who call for redressing the imbalance. Thus too the emphasis on resolving the problems of the Middle East as a way out of our predicament, problems that will remain when our predicament—whatever its issue—is all but forgotten.

3

It is almost with a sense of relief that one turns to the direct and altogether candid statement of resignation by Walter Levy in his remarkable *Foreign Affairs* essay, "Oil

and the Decline of the West." Levy's renown as a petro-
leum consultant, his long-standing acquaintance with
Middle East problems, and his record of prescience in
analyzing the oil crisis entitle him to be listened to with
great respect.

Not known for overstatement, Levy provides a bleak
estimate of our predicament in the Persian Gulf and of
our prospects for coping with the dangers confronting us.
From every perspective he considers, Levy concludes that
there has been a marked deterioration in the economic,
financial, and strategic position of the Western world
consequent upon the oil crisis. The financial problems of
recycling petrodollars at current OPEC prices, let alone at
future prices that may equal or exceed the rate of inflation, have become increasingly onerous. The circumstances that facilitated recycling in the years 1974
through 1978 can no longer be relied on. The problem
that preoccupied economists at the outset of the oil
crisis—how can the world pay for OPEC oil—has re-
turned with a vengeance. Levy thinks it unlikely that "our
national and international financial system can cope with
this problem without risking sustained recessions, a slow
rate—if any—of economic growth, high rates of inflation, widespread unemployment, industrial and national
bankruptcies, and political upheavals."

All this still assumes that the security and availability
of oil supplies—particularly Persian Gulf supplies—can
be relied on. But this assumption has now been called into serious question. The terms now imposed by producing countries for oil supplies increasingly include political
and other extraneous conditions that if not met may lead

to a cut off in supplies. Even if all economic and political terms are met, producers may and have arbitrarily changed the terms on which supplies are granted to consumers. Thus we have entered

> a period in international oil . . . where the producing countries can have it nearly all their way, because there are no countervailing powers they have to consider. The only question they have to face is whether, because of their own interest in the economic and political well-being of their customers, it would be prudent for them to exercise self-restraint.

This one-sided relationship might yet be remedied by a coordinated policy of resistance on the part of the major consumers. So far, Levy shows, they have acted in the spirit of *sauve qui peut* and of submission.

To these now familiar threats to the security and availability of oil supplies must be added those resulting from the internal instability of most Middle East regimes (exacerbated by rapid modernization), the many intraregional conflicts, and the growing Soviet political-military presence. Levy thinks it unlikely that any of these dangers can be effectively countered, in terms of securing vital oil supplies, by the West. The forces of internal instability will work their inexorable way. The disruption of oil supplies they will give rise to is seen as beyond our capacity to affect in any significant manner.

In this respect, the Carter Doctrine and the efforts it may or may not presage can have no more than peripheral bearing on future events in the Gulf. While Levy concedes that it was "absolutely necessary to state clearly our overwhelming interest in Persian Gulf oil," he finds the "real value" of the Carter Doctrine "based on the hope that the Doctrine will be accepted as credible and prove to be a deterrent to the Soviet Union—and will thus never be tested." As a means of addressing the threats held out by intraregional conflicts and by internal political instability, he considers the Carter Doctrine to be virtually worthless. It promises to involve us in the "most difficult and probably impossible assignment" of protecting the status quo in the Gulf at a time when the status quo is under increasing challenge, and to do so in circumstances where "we will probably never know whether or not there was any Soviet direct or indirect involvement." Even if we were better equipped than we are to carry out this assignment, it would not matter a great deal since the use of force in the Gulf would be self-defeating. "The one thing that seems to be certain is that if fighting in the Persian Gulf should erupt, the first targets that will be destroyed either by foreign or local forces, are the vital oil facilities."

Why should not these same considerations also largely negate the value of the Carter Doctrine as a credible deterrent to the Soviet Union? It turns out that Levy believes they do. "In terms of achieving U.S. policy objectives," he writes, "the Carter Doctrine might in the end prove to be as ineffective as was the Nixon Doctrine policy of the 1970s."

The Spenglerian prospects Levy holds out might be largely discounted either if the critical need for the oil of the Gulf could be substantially lessened in the years ahead or if all parties — producers and consumers, super-power rivals, et cetera — determined to behave coopera-tively and to take full account of each other's vital in-terests. But the oil dependency will persist for at least a long generation, and the utopian fantasy of cooperation is just that. Thus Levy's conclusion that

> we will probably be confronted by a series of major oil crises [that] . . . will set back world progress for many, many years. . . . [The] world, as we know it now, will probably not be able to maintain its cohesion, nor be able to provide for the continued economic progress of the people against the on-slaught of future oil shocks — with all that this might imply for the political stability of the West, its free institutions, and its internal and external security.

Plainly, the Levy message is one of sheer resignation. That it is brilliantly constructed and candidly put forth cannot detract from the outlook of despair and passivity it conveys. It may be that Levy believes his message, if taken to heart, will have a quite different effect, that it will shock his readers to serious thought about our predica-ment and eventually help to resolute action. If this is the intent it is skillfully obscured. The message that does come through with striking force is that our situation is for all practical purposes hopeless, and that there is little to be done but to resign ourselves to it and to face a for-bidding future with what equanimity we can. The effects of Levy's message are very similar to Hoffmann's, and this irrespective of the considerable differences that otherwise separate them.

4

It is instructive to recall that at each stage of the gathering crisis, the advocates of passivity have occupied what appeared to be the prudent and "sensible" position. In 1974–75 the response to the crisis, centered then as today in the Persian Gulf, divided in the main between those who argued that there was no need to consider the reassertion of Western power in order to preserve vital interests, and those who argued that although the need might exist, adequate and effective means for such reassertion did not. The former position commands much less support today than it once did; the latter position is now increasingly appealed to and enjoys broad favor. This is not surprising since our relative power position has markedly declined in the intervening years. If we were disadvantaged then, as so many vehemently insisted, what are we today? If we now look back almost with nostalgia on our circumstances of 1974–75, is it possible that in 1985 we may look back with similar nostalgia on our circumstances of today?

If there is a lesson to be learned from the past six years, it is that measures to redress an ever more adverse position in the Persian Gulf region must begin from where we are and not from where we would like to be when undertaking what is admittedly a difficult and dangerous task. We may never arrive at where we would like to be, whether because where we would like to be is a reason regularly invoked for postponing doing much of anything, or because while we are moving toward where we would like to be in order to act, others are moving as well. Surely we cannot safely proceed on the assumption—or rather the hope—that others will oblige us either by not moving at all or by moving at a relatively slower pace. Yet this is the assumption that some appear driven to make. While they are clear on the need to redress the present imbalance, they are also adamant on the need to avoid any action that might be seen by a militarily superior adversary as threatening or provocative.

Thus Paul Nitze has argued that since the present "correlation of forces" clearly is unfavorable to us, and whatever our efforts it will remain so for the next five years at least, we must learn to conduct strategy from relative weakness.* Given our position of vulnerability, we must take a leaf from the communist book. The object of policy, he has argued, "should be to throw dust in the enemy's eyes while getting on with reversing the trends and making them positive." But will the opponent permit us to make effective use of this expedient, the purpose of which he must be expected to recognize only too well, while otherwise remaining passive? Nitze doubts whether "there are *any* circumstances under which it

---

*Paul H. Nitze, "Policy and Strategy from Weakness," in *National Security in the 1980s: From Weakness to Strength,* ed. W. Scott Thompson (San Francisco: Institute for Contemporary Studies, 1980), pp. 443–56.

would be wise for the United States actually to commit military forces in combat with Soviet forces on the periphery of the European landmass."* If his admonition is well taken, however, one must also question whether there are any circumstances under which it would be wise for the United States to take measures the Soviets might find threatening or provocative—above all, measures taken to redress our position of vulnerability in the Persian Gulf region. In Nitze's assessment, the American position today in the Gulf resembles the Soviet position at the time of the Cuban missile crisis in 1962. A preponderant Soviet position at the conventional level is further supported at the strategic level by Soviet escalation control. In Nitze's words: "Soviet nuclear predominance carries the implied threat of an ability to escalate a conflict up the nuclear ladder just as the U.S. predominance in the Cuban missile crisis . . . implied such a threat to the Soviet Union."

What conclusions follow from this estimate? One is, as Nitze warns, that in the present situation "we understand our limitations and the constraints on our use of military

---

*Even more pointedly, he writes: "If the choice in solving our energy problem were to be viewed as one between using force in the Middle East or going without Middle East oil imports, the latter would clearly be the better choice." Given the dependence of Europe and Japan, our choice—if it be that—would issue in their necessity.

power." But the critical issue is what this understanding means in the present circumstances and where, if followed, it is likely to take us. Nitze's answer is that "there is no inherent reason, save a willful—and we hope unlikely—desire of the Soviet Union to confront us militarily in the near future, why we as a nation cannot conduct policy from an honest appraisal of our current position while refashioning our policies and forces and thus improve our position eventually to an honest parity."

It is a mystifying conclusion, given both the analysis that has preceded it and Nitze's known views about the continuing utility of military power. The Soviet purpose in seeking a favorable "correlation of forces" is not "to confront us militarily," but to attain certain political ends largely by virtue of enjoying an advantageous military position. Moscow hopes that these ends will be secured in the shadow of preponderant military power. If not, the defenders of a status quo that the Soviets wish to alter will eventually have to be confronted. Otherwise, what is the point of military power that is so largely disproportionate to defensive purposes? One may certainly argue over the nature of the ends Moscow seeks. But even if we accept the Hoffmann dictum of what "any serious analysis of Soviet policies and statements reveals," we are left with the Soviet insistence upon "equal rights and equal say" and a willingness to make use of such advantages as Moscow disposes of to achieve this end. Nitze does not so restrict Soviet policy aspirations. Yet he sees no inherent reason why we cannot use the present period to improve a position which, if openly challenged in the Persian Gulf, would have to be conceded. If this is indeed the case, there may be little policy left to conduct while we go about improving our military position.

The difficulty with Nitze's position is that there is no apparent connection between his strategic estimate, together with his general appreciation of Soviet policy, and the consequences he finds likely to follow from this estimate and appreciation. One can sympathize with the reluctance to draw the altogether grim consequences that would appear to follow. Even so, this reluctance has the effect of creating a startling disjuncture between the estimate made of our predicament today and the consequences held likely to follow from the estimate. If the estimate is reasonably accurate, passivity can be the only prudent response to further challenges in the Persian Gulf in the years ahead. That such passivity is for Nitze a necessary means of improving our strategic position rather than an end in itself (as it has been during the past decade and as many still wish it to be), cannot alter the conclusion that the intermediate term consequences are the same. On the other hand, the refusal to accept this conclusion and, instead, to hold out the likely prospect of being granted a period of grace, during which we may, in Nitze's words, "refashion our policies and forces and thus improve our position eventually to an honest parity," can only have the effect of casting serious doubt on the estimate made of our predicament.

Is the present danger as critical as the Nitze estimate would lead us to believe? The question is not put for rhetorical purposes. Even the Hoffmanns concede that there *is* a danger. And if they find an important part of this danger to stem from "oversimplifying and hysterical interpretations of Soviet behavior," they also concede a good part of the case on which the estimate of Nitze and other domestic "adversaries" rests. It is Hoffmann, after all, who speaks of the "enormous military advantages" enjoyed by the Soviet Union in the region of the Persian Gulf, just as it is Hoffmann who acknowledges that Soviet ambitions "threaten our strategic, economic, and political positions."

Indeed, in one important respect Hoffmann goes further than many of his domestic adversaries in depicting the gravity of the danger. He characterizes the Soviet interest in the Gulf in the same terms that he characterizes the interest of the West and Japan. Fortunately, his characterization overstates the Soviet interest. If it did not, and if the Soviets possess the advantages there that Hoffmann admits they do, then the conclusion forces itself that the danger is even greater than the Nitzes appear to believe.

The view that we are roughly in the same strategic position today that the Soviets were at the time of the Cuban missile crisis rests upon three assumptions. One appears indisputable: the very considerable imbalance in conventional forces favoring Moscow. Another is very much disputed: Soviet nuclear predominance. Still another is quite misplaced: the balance or equality of interest the two superpowers have in the Gulf. Today, as in 1962, it is the United States that enjoys the relative advantage in the balance of interest, if only by virtue of the defensive position this country has occupied, whether earlier in the Caribbean or at present in the Persian Gulf.

In the case of the Persian Gulf, the predominance of the American interest is all the more apparent and compelling. While it may be argued that a very different outcome of the Cuban missile crisis—one that enabled the Soviets to keep Cuba as a missile base—would not have resulted in the disintegration of the American position in Europe, it is clearly implausible to argue that Soviet control of the Gulf could have any other result. By confronting us in the Gulf, the Soviets would in effect confront us in Europe. By threatening our position in the Gulf, the Soviets would in effect threaten our position in Europe. Indeed, this hemisphere apart, by threatening our position in the Gulf, the Soviets would in effect threaten our position everywhere.

There is no "equality of interest" between the West and the USSR in the region of the Gulf, and it is dangerously misleading to assert otherwise. What to Europe is indispensable to its economic life, and to the United States is indispensable to its entire position in the world outside this hemisphere, is indispensable to the Soviet Union as the key to global predominance. Without that key, Moscow would still be able to expand its position and influence in the world. But without that same key, Washington would have surrendered almost entirely its post–World War II position.

This asymmetry in interest is usually taken to imply a disparity in willingness to incur risks in the event of confrontation. In the Cuban missile crisis the side thus favored also happened to be the side possessing relative military advantage at both the conventional and strategic nuclear levels. In a confrontation over control of the Gulf, would the loss of the latter advantage cancel out the advantage conferred by possession of the greater, and even compelling, interest? Clearly, it would do so if the Soviet Union enjoyed the same decisive advantage at the strategic nuclear level that it is acknowledged on almost all sides to possess at the level of conventional forces. However, it is the persisting doubt and uncertainty on this point that does not permit discounting the significance of the imbalance of interest. It is the same doubt and uncertainty that requires treating with caution the parallel drawn between 1962 and today.

5

Even if our position in the Persian Gulf today does not present us with a Cuban missile crisis in reverse, it is surely serious enough. Among those who believe much greater efforts can and must be made, there are nevertheless differences in view over what we should endeavor to do. We have already noted Nitze's counsel that we must strive to attain an "honest parity" and that there is no good alternative to such a policy. In much the same vein, Albert Wohlstetter urges the "broad alternative of meeting a conventional threat on its own terms."

Certainly, these prescriptions are unexceptionable when judged in terms of desirability. But are they possible of realization, particularly in the next five to seven years? The critical issue confronting us is not the position we will be in by the late 1980s, important though this undoubtedly is, but how we will get to the late 1980s without courting disaster.

Whereas Nitze believes we can only get there by exercising extreme prudence and, though he does not explicitly so say, by luck, Wohlstetter thinks a viable conventional defense of the Gulf is possible even within this intermediate period.* The elements of such a defense, he argues, "require not merely a force rapidly deployed from the United States" but also "a continuous and politically tolerable allied combat presence . . . able to defend itself against land-based air attack and yet project enough firepower ashore to deter, delay, or disrupt an initial adversary surprise attack aimed at seizing key points on the gulf." While the delay must be long enough to permit bringing in reinforcements by air, "the firepower and the presence required can be more modest if it is available very early" because an attacking Soviet force presumably would have many vulnerabilities. Thus a "greatly increased naval combat presence, able to defend itself and to project power ashore" would form the core of the presence capable of disrupting an attack and giving time for a rapid deployment force to bring in reinforcements. In

---

*Albert Wohlstetter, "Half-Wars and Half-Policies in the Persian Gulf," *National Security in the 1980s,* ed. W. Scott Thompson, pp. 164–70.

time, such a force would restore our credibility with the states in the area, offer them evidence for believing we could protect them against attack (whether from the Soviet Union, radical neighbors, or radical factions), and perhaps make them more willing to offer land facilities for alliance use. This, in turn, would be likely to open the way to stationing a "land presence as well, or at least an increased use of land bases in a crisis."

The Wohlstetter view is that it is quite possible to meet a conventional threat on its own terms, and that this can be done by a substantial increase in present efforts along lines indicated above. At the same time, he is quite emphatic in rejecting reliance on nuclear escalation for these reasons:

> The threat of using nuclear weapons in response to a conventional incursion — of introducing a trip wire or plateglass defense of the Persian Gulf — is likely to frighten allies, especially those in the region, more than it will the Russians. A nuclear tripwire defense in the European center becomes progressively less persuasive as Soviet nuclear strength increases at short, medium, and intercontinental range. A tripwire in the Persian Gulf is likely to be even less persuasive. In general, a tripwire policy does not register a determination to use nuclear weapons in time of crisis; rather, it registers a lack of will before the crisis to prepare to meet a nonnuclear threat on its own terms.

Whether Wohlstetter's strictures on threatening the use of nuclear weapons are well taken is one thing; quite another is whether a nonnuclear threat can be effectively dealt with on its own terms. Wohlstetter does not really argue, let alone plausibly demonstrate, that it can. What he does argue is the need for a force that, in his words, "could so increase the risks to an aggressor as to discourage him from attacking." Are the risks those of being repelled, of suffering defeat in the Gulf, and this regardless of the magnitude of the conventional incursion? Wohlstetter does not claim this and for good reason. The force he advocates is one that may deter and, should deterrence fail, defend against certain kinds of conventional threats. But it is not against any and all such threats that the force can hold out the promise of effective defense.

At issue here is not the desirability of meeting a conventional threat on its own terms, so far as this is possible, but whether a defense of the Gulf is possible against the kind of incursion the Soviets could make if they were so determined. There seems little prospect that such defense is feasible. Certainly it is not in the critical period immediately ahead. We must recognize that we cannot defend the Gulf against a determined Soviet assault — not now, not in the immediate years ahead, and perhaps not ever. Beyond a certain level of conventional threat, we must either rely on the threat of responding with nuclear weapons or concede that there is no response we can make.

The case against relying on a nuclear tripwire in the Persian Gulf gains in persuasiveness by assuming that it is intended as a substitute for making a serious effort to strengthen conventional capability in the region. A strategy that relies on nuclear deterrence to the virtual exclusion of conventional defense not only encounters the now familiar problems of credibility, but when applied to the Gulf it also meets the further difficulty that arises from the variety of circumstances that are absent in Europe but that largely define the condition of the Gulf. These familiar circumstances could well mean, as Wohlstetter points out, that the West might have the burden of initiating military action. Yet in these circumstances, a nuclear tripwire would either lack credibility or simply prove irrelevant.

What follows from these considerations is that the threat of nuclear escalation in a Gulf strategy must be limited to deterring a major Soviet assault and to minimizing the otherwise corrosive effects the threat of such assault might have over time. A tripwire policy in the Gulf cannot be expected to carry greater persuasiveness than it does in Europe. It cannot enjoy even a roughly comparable persuasiveness if it does not have the requisite conventional force underpinning. Intensity of interest alone cannot substitute for the commitment that must be given expression in conventional forces. Moreover, what limited experience we have points to the need for a substantial ground presence if a nuclear threat is to carry the requisite credibility. It does so for the reason that such presence insures, in a way air and naval forces cannot, that an attack on the area in question will result in a conflict that reinforces a threat, the carrying out of which admittedly may defy rational considerations.

The argument here is not one of rejecting a conventional defense and relying instead on a tripwire policy. It is one of embracing both the need for a conventional defense and the need at some point for a tripwire policy. The essential goal of a viable strategy in the Persian Gulf is to fashion a conventional force structure that can effectively deal with all contingencies that may arise short of a determined Soviet assault, and that will also make such assault an extremely dangerous move by virtue of the level of conventional conflict it would necessarily entail. That level of conflict must in turn raise the meaningful prospect of nuclear escalation, a prospect we can—and should—no more attempt to disavow in the Persian Gulf than in Europe.

6

If we could achieve this goal we would immeasurably improve our present position. As matters stand, we are very far from doing so. Nor are the prospects for achieving it promising so long as the Carter Doctrine remains indicative of the broad outlines of policy in the Persian Gulf, and the current strategy persists for deploying conventional military power in the Gulf.

The Carter Doctrine acknowledges our vital interest in the Gulf and declares our determination to repel by any means necessary, including military force, an attempt by an outside force to gain control of the region. The declaration is directed at the Soviet Union, since it is the only nation that represents an outside force capable of gaining control of the Persian Gulf.

The "determination" expressed in the Carter Doctrine is one of countering Soviet expansion in the Persian Gulf.

Yet it is not only Soviet expansion that may jeopardize Western interests in this area. One might persuasively argue that the principal threat to these interests in the future will come from the same forces that have formed the principal threat in the recent past. These forces have been "inside" the Persian Gulf region, not "outside." It is true that our response in past years to these inside forces has been conditioned in part by the growing strength of the outside force and our fear of confrontation with it. However, a policy that has made one concession after the other to the oil-producing countries of the Gulf has been motivated by considerations quite distinct from a fear of confrontation. Very little will have been learned from this costly policy of appeasement if it is seen in retrospect simply, or even primarily, as a function of the Soviet-American relationship.

In addressing itself exclusively to the threat held out by the Soviet Union, the Carter Doctrine leaves unaddressed the other continuing threat. This omission reflects something more than the desire to avoid the charge that American policy is now committed to intervention on behalf of the status quo—a charge that has been made in any event. At root, the form in which the Carter Doctrine is cast reflects the persisting doubt and uncertainty over the circumstances justifying the employment of force in the Persian Gulf region. This doubt and uncertainty must account in large measure for the ambiguity of purpose that marks the Carter Doctrine. Directed as it ostensibly is only against any Soviet attempt to gain control of the Persian Gulf, the Carter Doctrine obscures what should be the central purpose of policy, to preserve access to the oil supplies of the Gulf. It is because Soviet expansion into the Gulf threatens this interest that any such attempt must be opposed. To the degree that developments indigenous to the Gulf, or very nearly so, threaten this same interest, they too must be opposed. This is the logic dictated by interest. But the United States has been unwilling to accept this logic.

The Carter Doctrine has found military expression in the stationing of a fleet in the Arabian Sea; in stationing cargo ships at Diego Garcia that would support a Marine Corps brigade of 12,000 with weapons, ammunition, and supplies; in seeking air and naval "facilities" in Kenya, Somalia, Oman, and Egypt; and in building up a Rapid Deployment Force that is based in this country and is presumably designed to respond quickly, even preemptively, in the face of sudden threats arising in the Gulf region.

The common characteristic of these various measures is the avoidance, so far as possible, of an intimate relationship between the states of the region and American military forces. Even in the case of "facilities" that a limited number of states appear ready to grant, this euphemism is indicative of the reluctance to admit a relationship now regarded as a serious political liability and one to be avoided so far as possible, despite the fact that many of those who shun the American relationship have no alternative prospect of effectively defending themselves

101

against the Soviet Union or even against intraregional aggression. The American government has sought to make a virtue of the necessity thus imposed on it and to find advantages in a military disposition that is largely free of the many difficulties that result from alliance relationships and the possession of regular bases for air, naval, and particularly ground forces. In fact, these "advantages" largely define the dimensions of America's strategic dilemmas today in the Persian Gulf; they reflect the low estate to which American power has sunk in the region while making extraordinarily difficult attempts at the effective restoration of this power within a reasonable period of time.

Do the measures so far taken—above all, the Rapid Deployment Force—comprise an adequate response to the situation to which they are ostensibly addressed? Do they give credibility to the Carter Doctrine? If the answer depends on an existing military capability able to carry out the liberal promise of the Carter Doctrine—to repel an assault on the region by any outside force—the answer must almost certainly be a negative one. Given the conventional forces the Soviet Union can presently deploy on very short notice in the Gulf, there is no apparent way by which these forces could be repelled by conventional American military response. On this point there is virtual unanimity of judgment among military analysts.

Moreover, as already stated, very few believe the present imbalance of conventional forces can be overcome for at least several years, and this assuming that the interim period is used to full advantage. Many doubt that it can ever be overcome in the literal sense of having the capability of responding in time and with forces of sufficient magnitude to make good on the promise of the Carter Doctrine. On this view, the president's declaration cannot be taken literally as even a meaningful aspiration. Instead, the best that may be aspired to is a conventional capability that can impose risks of such magnitude as to discourage an aggressor from attacking.

It has been intimated that these risks are already imposed on the Soviet Union by virtue of the forces the United States has ready to oppose a Soviet incursion in the Gulf. But this claim is widely doubted. The naval forces in the Arabian Sea are considered by experts as insufficient for the tasks they would have to perform. These forces must be able not only to defend themselves against a land-based air attack, which they are presently incapable of doing, but also to disrupt an attacking force with sufficient effectiveness to permit enough time for deploying ground forces. Even if these requirements could be met, the interventionary force would have to be of a magnitude that exceeds by far the present Rapid Deployment Force.

The problems attending the Rapid Deployment Force have generated a great deal of discussion and controversy. Where the experts disagree on so many points, the amateur must proceed with care. The effectiveness of the force will depend upon the rapidity with which it can be deployed and the size. Even if a very small force can be deployed very rapidly, the size of the force must severely limit the missions it can accomplish. On the other hand, a substantial force that can only be deployed over an extended period sacrifices its raison d'etre. Finally, assuming the requirements of rapidity and size could be achieved, the force would still meet with disaster should it not possess the logistical tail for sustained operations.

These requirements impose formidable obstacles if it is assumed that the capabilities and proximity of Soviet forces to the Gulf enable it to mount a large operation in a very brief period. Many do not grant this assumption, particularly the time element. Instead of hours, it is argued, we are likely to have a warning period of at least several days, if not weeks. But military plans cannot safely be made by taking optimistic assumptions. Moreover, the longer the period of warning, the more ambiguous and uncertain it is likely to be, and thus the more reluctant American officials might be to deploy the force. The possible brevity of the warning period creates severe problems in the absense of forces on the scene that can disrupt and delay an attack, since even if the means exist for transporting a force from its American base, the time required for transport may prove fatal.

This difficulty apart, the American defense establishment does not possess the capability to airlift within a very few days a substantial force — let us say, a division — along with the heavy military equipment it would require for sustained operations. This equipment might be pre-positioned on either land or at sea. But with the possible exception of Egypt, the other candidates for providing facilities have so far refused to permit the pre-positioning of such equipment, which has in turn required a maritime pre-positioning program that is both costly and more vulnerable to attack. Only in a crisis could the United States use facilities to land the large cargo planes now planned. This arrangement leaves open the questions of capability and time, and the even more basic question of the political reliability of the countries according us facilities though not permanent leases. It would be rash to assume that the use of such facilities will be unrelated to the circumstances attending a crisis, not to speak of the nature of the regimes that might be in power at the time.

This is by no means an exhaustive inventory of the principal difficulties besetting the Rapid Deployment Force. It suffices, however, to support the conclusion that for at least several critical years this force — our principal reliance in dealing with the contingencies that may await us — will remain quite modest in size. In favorable circumstances, it might be employed to forestall undesirable political change in an important, though militarily weak, oil-producing state. This change may or may not involve the Soviet Union, whether directly or indirectly. It may well be that at the time we are required to act we will not know the extent, if any, of Soviet involvement.

Thus the principal contingency the Rapid Deployment Force might respond to is the kind that the Carter Doctrine does not address, and the one over which the United States continues to manifest a great deal of indecision. The qualification *might* must be emphasized for other reasons. The Rapid Deployment Force is not visible to the states of the Gulf. It is something that must be imagined. This represents a considerable liability and not an asset as is so commonly assumed. For American power no longer commands much respect in the region. If a measure of the respect American power used to command is to be restored, there must be a visible demonstration of this power, and the more impressive the demonstration the better. The restoration of American status and credibility must begin with the local states of the Persian Gulf region that have managed to outmaneuver and to intimidate Western powers for a decade.

7

These difficulties marking our present efforts are not inexorable. They are not dictated by either geography or the logic of military power. They are, for the most part, preeminently political. The prevailing view is that though our difficulties are political in nature, they cannot be altered, and certainly not in the immediate period ahead. This view is regularly advanced with all the certitude that other views about what is and is not possible to do in the region have been advanced in recent years. Given the sorry record of a policy that has largely reflected these views, it does not seem unreasonable to question what passes as the received wisdom today on the political constraints held to condition — indeed, to dictate — military strategy.

One thing seems clear. There is no apparent way by which we can conform to these constraints and effectively respond to the deepening crisis in the Gulf. This being so, we must choose either to resign ourselves to a future over which we can have but little control, or attempt to break out of the constraints that hamper a more effective response than is presently being made.

The principal constraint results from the absence of regular bases that would permit the permanent stationing of land-based aircraft and ground forces. Ideally, these bases and forces should be located in the immediate area that must be defended, whether against a hostile coup, intraregional aggression, or a Soviet incursion. But the immediate area that must be defended — Saudi Arabia — is also the area considered least willing and least able to receive foreign forces. Short of this ideal, the next best alternative is the possession of regular bases and the positioning of air and ground forces on the immediate periphery of the Gulf, where they may still be considered as something closely akin to a preemptive presence.

If this next best alternative is to be realized, it can be done only with the cooperation of the two states on which a visible American policy in the Middle East will depend in the period ahead: Egypt and Israel.* In the northern Sinai there are the bases that can support the forces required for an American air and ground presence that, once in place, might radically alter our present position of vulnerability in the Gulf. According to the terms of the peace treaty between Egypt and Israel, these bases — Eitam and Etzion — must be turned over to the Egyptians prior to the final Israeli withdrawal from the Sinai in Spring 1982. Before turning them over for Egyptian "civilian use," the Israelis are entitled to destroy, as they did in 1980 at Refidim in the Southern Sinai, the complex infrastructure that required years to construct and without which the bases have but little military utility. As matters now stand, two of the best bases in the entire Middle East — one providing access to a port on the Medi-

---

*The proposal sketched out in these pages was written in early Fall 1980. Since its initial formulation, events appear to have overtaken it. Then, too, it has been subject to a good deal of criticism, primarily on the grounds that it is unacceptable to Egypt and that, even if it were acceptable, it would further alienate Egypt from other Arab states, primarily Saudi Arabia. I remain unpersuaded by these arguments. At the time these lines are written (March 1981), Egypt has yet to be approached with the requisite seriousness. As for the Saudi reaction, it rests on the misplaced assumption that a show of determination by the United States, here in conjunction with Egypt, would alienate the Saudis, whereas the prospects are that such show would have precisely the opposite effects. It is of course the case that the proposal urged here would not, if acted upon, resolve *all* of our problems. But nothing will, not even an American presence in Saudi Arabia. Indeed, such presence would probably still have to be supported by outlying bases, of which the Sinai bases would be invaluable.

terranean, both isolated from population centers, and both within less than 90 minutes flying time from the Gulf—will be rendered of negligible value for military purposes at a time when the American government is negotiating for limited rights of access to inferior bases both in Egypt and elsewhere.

The explanation given for this apparent madness is President Sadat's position, reiterated on a number of occasions, that Egypt must reclaim full sovereignty over the Sinai. Presumably, the American use of the Sinai bases would deny that claim, though why it should do so is left unclear. There is also the point made by Egyptian officials that the Israeli-built air bases in the Sinai are too sensitive politically to permit their use by American forces. But this point is not easy to follow unless it is simply a way of saying that the Egyptian government does not wish to appear to be compromising any of its rights to the Sinai. If so, it is only a variation on the sovereignty claim, and one that might be met in a number of ways.

The point has been made by many that even if Sadat could be persuaded to agree to American use of the Sinai bases, the consequences of such agreement for his domestic position might prove to be disastrous. To permit the stationing of American troops on Egyptian soil, it is argued, could strip the present government of its legitimacy. Sadat would appear as an instrument of the United States and the betrayer of Egyptian independence. When applied to some Persian Gulf states, the argument carries some weight. When applied to

Egypt, it must be met with skepticism. There was a time not so many years ago when the presence of thousands of Soviet advisors and military personnel—stationed, it may be added, near population centers—did not deprive an Egyptian government of its legitimacy. Why should an American presence have such effect, particularly one that would be stationed in so remote an area and that—as we shall presently note—could help to implement the provisions of a treaty that has restored Egyptian territory?

Nor is this all. If the regular presence of American forces on Egyptian territory would have the consequences many believe they so clearly discern, why would not the temporary presence of forces have a similar effect? Evidently it would if this argument is to be believed. If so, the Egyptian officials are either fools and digging their own graves by permitting the Americans the use of facilities such as the Red Sea port of Ras Banas even for "certain limited purposes," or, despite their assurances, they have no intention of permitting the use of facilities in periods of crisis (a use that is reported to include the temporary stationing of ground forces). Since neither assumption seems very plausible it is not unreasonable to conclude that the argument is a case of special pleading—clearly with respect to Egypt and very likely with respect to a number of other states in the region as well.

Although an American ground presence in the northern Sinai must be justified primarily in relation to its impact on our position in the Gulf, there would likely be important collateral advantages to be gained by its introduction. These advantages bear on the implementation of the Egyptian-Israeli peace treaty and, beyond the peace treaty, on the prospects for progress on the Palestinian issue. The Israeli withdrawal from the Sinai is conditioned upon the establishment of certain security arrangements, part of which must be carried out either by a United Nations force or, should the establishment of such force prove impossible, by a multinational force acceptable to Egypt and Israel. It is now apparent that there will be no United Nations force due to the opposition of the Soviet Union. In its place, a multinational force could be formed in which the United States would assume the predominant role. Indeed, there is no reason why such a force could not be made up from Egyptian, Israeli, and American contingents.

The need to implement the provisions of the peace treaty thus provides the opportunity to introduce a permanent American military presence in the Sinai. The stability of this presence could be insured by the need to obtain the agreement of both parties to the treaty as a condition for its removal. It is evident that the force required to implement the arrangements called for in the treaty is not the force required to meet various contingencies that may arise in the Persian Gulf. On the other hand, there is nothing to prevent the parties from agreeing to an Americana contribution that is quite disproportionate to the needs of the peace treaty alone. Put more candidly, there is nothing to prevent the parties from using the treaty as a means to introcuce a substantial American military presence, whether immediately or in stages.

In a broader perspective, the impact of a permanent and substantial American presence on the peace process can be no more than speculative. At the very least, however, the arrangement here suggested would go very far toward guaranteeing the peace that must provide the cornerstone for any general settlement of the Arab-Israeli conflict. Nor is it farfetched to consider that the effects of an American presence would go a good deal further. A permanent American commitment in the Sinai could in time affect the outlook of both Israel and Jordan toward the Palestinian issue. What may presently seem to both parties an insoluble issue may take on a different appearance should an American presence become a reliable given in their calculations. After all, it was not so long ago that an American guarantee was seen by many observers in this country as the key that might turn the lock to an otherwise intractable conflict. This a guarantee could never do. Instead, the lock had first to be turned by others, as indeed it was turned by the dramatic sequence of events that began in late 1977. Once turned, however, the idea of a guarantee — or, in the form suggested here, its functional equivalent — may well become relevant, and this despite the indifference shown toward it today by those who were formerly its ardent supporters.

At the same time, it must be emphasized that the need for an American military presence in the northern Sinai cannot be justified primarily in terms of its prospective impact on the peace process. Even if the impact were to prove negligible, unlikely though this must be, the need would remain undiminished. A settlement of the Arab-Israeli conflict is an interest that cannot be compared in importance with the Western interest in insuring access to the oil supplies of the Persian Gulf. Were it not for the connection mistakenly drawn between the two, a connection made more insistently today than ever, the West would have the same modest concern with the Palestinian issue that it had a decade ago. Indeed, were it not for the obsessive illusion that a settlement of the Palestinian problem can provide our deliverance in the Persian Gulf, we would by now have been forced to confront the stark choice before us in the Gulf. Instead, the hope persists that the choice between conceding vital interests and moving resolutely to restore the dangerous imbalance can be avoided by a settlement of the Arab-Israeli conflict.

The choice cannot be avoided. If vital interests are not to be conceded, with consequences even pessimists blanch at when considering, countervailing power will have to be applied and soon. Yet there is no apparent way this can be effectively done while adhering to the constraints that at present define our efforts.

The breaking of these constraints would not remove the dangers we face today in the Persian Gulf. A policy compounded in equal measures of inadvertence and fear has succeeded in bringing us to a point where there is now no safe way out of our predicament. Still, an extremely precarious position could be substantially improved by the introduction of a permanent land and air presence of size, support, and proximity to the Gulf to deal with most contingencies that might arise. There can be no assurance that the force would be employed should the need arise. But this is only to say that there can be no assurance that the prevailing policy of a decade will be once and for all abandoned. Without the required instruments to support a new policy, however, the time may well be drawing near when a change in policy will have become all but impossible.

V

The Two Containments: An Argument Retraced

1

The general view taken in these pages rests on the assumption that the principal security interests of the United States have remained remarkably constant since World War II. Thus the American vital interest in Western Europe and Japan remains essentially unaltered. That interest requires the maintenance of an overall balance of power that has now been placed in jeopardy by the Soviet buildup of both strategic and conventional arms. That interest also requires the assurance of accesss to those raw materials on which the health of the economies of the United States, Western Europe, and Japan depend. This assurance of access is now seriously challenged in the Persian Gulf.

The loss of these interests would not jeopardize America's physical security as such. Quite the contrary: our physical security can likely be jeopardized today only through their pursuit, as it is only through nuclear attack that our physical existence as a nation can be placed in question.

If our security interests and our aspirations as a great power did not extend beyond the North American continent, the prospect of our ever being attacked by the Soviet Union would be virtually nonexistent. No matter how relatively advantaged their strategic forces might be, the Soviets would still have to incure terrible risks in attacking us. In a world where we would no longer contest them, what incentive would they have to take such risks? An America that defined its vital interests in terms that did not extend beyond this continent would be an America that placed its physical security in least jeopardy.*

It is curious that this all important point is still so commonly overlooked or misunderstood. Discussions of security continue to reflect conditions that have not obtained for more than a generation. These discussions continue to reflect the calculations relevant to a conventional—that

---

*This is the principal reason urged on behalf of an isolationist policy today. Thus Earl C. Ravenal writes, with respect to Western Europe and the Persian Gulf, that: "Ironically, because the cases America cares about most are also most demanding and possibly terminal, they are the ones the United States would in fact—and should in principle—shrink from defending." "Doing Nothing," *Foreign Policy* (Summer 1980), p. 36.

is, a prenuclear—balance-of-power system. In such a system, even a great power had to be constantly concerned over possible threats to its physical security, and this despite the absence of contention with other great powers over interests each sought to control. In such a system, as Walter Lippmann once argued, "to be isolated is for any state the worst of all possible predicaments."* It was the worst of all possible predicaments for the reason that a surfeit of defensive and deterrent power was practically unachievable.

In theory, the possibility existed for one state to acquire a degree of power sufficient to deter attack by any other state or combination of states. In practice, though, this ideal condition was seldom, if ever, achieved. It was primarily for this reason, Lippmann contended, that we had to abandon isolationism and form alliances with the states of the Old World. A hostile state, or combination of states, in control of Eurasia would possess a potential military strength far greater than what we might muster. We would not only be forced back to this hemisphere, it would even be doubtful that we could continue indefinitely to defend the North American continent. Assuming that we sought to avoid contention with the masters of the Old World, they could nevertheless seek to embrace contention with us. Given the resources at their

---

*Walter Lippmann, *U.S. Foreign Policy: Shield of the Republic* (Boston: Little, Brown, 1943), p. 105.

disposal, Lippmann and others believed, they might well prove successful in their efforts. Even if they could not undertake the actual conquest of this country, they could achieve a position of military superiority sufficient to tempt them to attack the North American continent.

Whatever the merits of this argument as applied to the United States in the 1930s and 1940s, it has little if any merit today. This is so because nuclear-missile weapons have changed what was before virtually a law of international politics. Since the great nuclear power can now destroy any other state or combination of states, nuclear-missile weapons have conferred what had heretofore proven unachievable: a surfeit of deterrent power.

It is indeed the case that in the extreme situation the great nuclear power is absolutely vulnerable with respect to its great adversary. But this ultimate vulnerability cannot be significantly reduced — let alone removed — by any alliance the great nuclear power may form. Nor can this vulnerability be significantly increased by the loss of allies. Our alliances do not contribute to our physical security. Instead, they constitute perhaps the principal threat to that security, since the prospect of using nuclear weapons is most likely to arise as a result of threats to their security.

If prevention of the one contingency that would clearly threaten America's survival as a nation formed the overriding objective of policy, American foreign policy might be expected to be quite different from what it is today. As against an adversary that is no longer strategically inferior

118

to us but, if anything, appears on the way to achieving a strategic advantage, we might be expected to disabuse both ourselves and our allies that we would risk nuclear war on behalf of anything other than the "national self," narrowly defined. A former secretary of state has attempted to do just that. In a situation of approximate strategic parity between the United States and the Soviet Union, Henry Kissinger declared in September 1979 to a NATO conference in Brussels, it is no longer realistic to believe that America's strategic forces can serve as a credible deterrent against a Soviet attack.* A candid commentator, Irving Kristol, has interpreted Kissinger's statement to mean that "the only function of our arsenal is to deter a Soviet first-strike against the United States itself — that and nothing else."†

Kristol considers this conclusion "quite obvious to everyone" by now. Is it? Is it quite obvious to the leaders of the Soviet Union that this government would not use strategic weapons save in response to an attack on the United States? One may seriously doubt that it is. That doubt, moreover, does not arise merely from a declaratory policy that, taken at face value, leaves the Kristol conclusion anything but obvious. It also arises from our actions. If the only function of our strategic forces is to deter a Soviet first-strike against the United States itself,

---

*Kissinger, *For the Record,* pp. 241–42.

†Irving Kristol, "NATO's Moment of Truth," *Wall Street Journal,* September 24, 1979, p. 30.

why should we worry as we do about a prospective Soviet capability to destroy our land-based missiles? It will not do to answer that we must worry about a Soviet counterforce capability for which we have no equivalent today. Why must we have an equivalent if the only function of our force is to respond to a Soviet attack?

Again it will not do to answer that we want to be in a position to threaten a response in kind to a Soviet counterforce threat, rather than to be limited to the option of threatening to destroy cities, a threat that may well place us at a grave disadvantage in some future confrontation with the Soviet Union. For if our strategic forces are now limited only to responding to a first strike, and this limitation is quite obvious to the Soviet Union, then why should we worry over a Soviet counterforce capability against which we may be unable to respond in kind? The Soviet leaders would have no temptation to use that capability against us, knowing that we would never strike at them first. Nor would they enjoy any particular advantage from such capability in a future confrontation. What advantage they might enjoy would instead derive simply from the possession of a conventional force superiority—a superiority that would not be offset by any lingering doubts over the possibility that at some point this country might resort to the use of its strategic forces in circumstances other than a direct attack against the United States itself.

It is another matter entirely to insist that in their role as a deterrent today, America's strategic forces no longer

have the credibility they once did. While this is undoubtedly the case, it does not follow that these forces are now
credible only as a deterrent against a direct attack on the
United States. Were this indeed the situation today, it
would signal a radical change in the American position.
Were we once to abandon extended deterrence, and to be
known to have abandoned it, we could no longer maintain anything resembling our postwar position in the
world. Allies and adversaries may doubt as they have
never doubted before whether extended deterrence remains a meaningful policy. But if doubt were once
replaced by the clear conviction that it was not, the ensuing change in the American position — whether in Western Europe or in the Persian Gulf — would be momentous.

Why should we persist in commitments whose sacrifice
would not risk our physical survival but whose retention
does? If nuclear war is the one contingency that may
threaten America's survival as a nation, why should we
run the risks entailed by this prospect over interests that if
lost would still not jeopardize survival? The answer, of
course, is that nations, particularly great nations, have
seldom been willing to equate their security with their
physical dimensions alone. Instead, it is taken for granted
that a nation's existence has dimensions other than the
merely physical dimensions, that the nation is something
much more than its physical attributes.

America has been no exception to this characteristic
manner of viewing security. Whether or not America

"survives" is not an issue that can be considered simply in terms of the attributes that make up the nation's physical person; it must also be considered in terms of a self whose identity requires the preservation of certain values and of the political, economic, and social institutions that embody these values. Even if the loss of areas deemed vital to security would not render America physically insecure, the result might still be expected to threaten the integrity of our institutions and seriously impair the quality of our domestic life. It is for this reason that the one threat to America's physical survival continues to be risked, whether it be for the protection of Western Europe or the oil supplies on which the economic life of our major allies depends.

There is no need to speculate on the consequences that would follow from a Western Europe that had fallen directly under the sway of the Soviet Union, or indirectly as a result of Soviet control of the Persian Gulf. These consequences would prove very serious, even if it is assumed that an America confined largely to this hemisphere would not require greater defense expenditures. It may be that the United States would be able to retain a market economy and enjoy a modest degree of economic growth in an international system largely dominated by the Soviet Union. These are very optimistic — indeed excessively optimistic — assumptions. But even if they are granted for the sake of argument, they still do not address the profound effects that would result from an America shut off from societies that begot and that continue to

122

nourish our culture and institutions, societies our affinity to which has deep moral and psychological significance.*

2

If this is the realm of necessity for American foreign policy today, what are the implications of responding to necessity? First and foremost, what kind of relationship can we reasonably expect to have with the Soviet Union? A candid answer is that the measures required to redress the arms balance, to strengthen the defense of Western Europe, and to improve the Western position in the Persian Gulf will strain our relationship with the Soviet Union in the foreseeable future. Other issues may also intervene to compound the difficulties and dangers that are now all too likely to mark the relationship. In any case, the outlook is bleak.

The principal reasons for this are clear enough. Moscow is likely to view a significant effort at rearmament as an attempt not merely to redress an arms balance, but to reestablish an overall position of superiority. Moreover, whatever the Soviet leaders may say about their determination to match any American effort, they are bound to entertain serious doubts over their ability to do so in the longer run. They may well be skeptical over the wil-

---

*These considerations are largely ignored by those like Earl Ravenal when considering the "acceptability of the costs of non-intervention." "Doing Nothing," pp. 35–39.

lingness of this nation to accept for long the sacrifices substantial rearmament would entail—certainly their skepticism finds ample support in the doubts entertained by many American observers. They must harbor, however, great apprehension over the results of our rearmament if given sustained public support. Even if the Soviet government were nevertheless willing and able to match the American effort, the result would severely strain their economy and might produce serious domestic unrest. Yet if Moscow should fail to respond to the American effort, the result, again in Soviet eyes, might be seen as the beginning of the end to pretensions of global power status.

These considerations alone provide ample grounds for pessimism. To them, however, must be added the structural causes for conflict that are provided by the Persian Gulf. The observation has been regularly made that the instability characteristic of much of the Third World provides the single most significant, and seemingly intractable, source of conflict between the United States and the Soviet Union. But it is not the points of contention and conflict *generally* in the Third World that have brought the superpowers into potentially dangerous confrontation today; it is the growing competition in the region of the Persian Gulf that has done so. It is the Gulf that forms the indispensable key to the defense of the American global position, just as it forms the indispensable key without which the Soviet Union cannot seriously aspire to global predominance. Alongside the stakes accruing from control of the Gulf, the contest in other regions of the Third World can have but peripheral significance.

The intrinsic importance of the Gulf thus acts as a magnet that, for different reasons, neither superpower can resist. The competition for control of the area is about as certain as anything can be in politics. So long as it persists — and it probably will for years to come — it will hold out the constant prospect for dangerous confrontations between the United States and the Soviet Union.

With the advantage of hindsight, a number of observers now find that this prospect might have been largely avoided had American policy accepted the Soviet Union as a partner in the Middle East peace process. Instead, by seeking to exclude Moscow from the Middle East settlement, we succeeded only in provoking renewed Soviet determination to improve its position in the areas around the Persian Gulf.

This argument, however, indicates an unwillingness to acknowledge that the Gulf cannot be bought by a policy conceding the form in the hope of retaining the substance. Quite apart from the notorious difficulties raised by including the Soviets in the peace process, how would this inclusion have diminished their aspirations in the Gulf? Presumably including them would have been an acknowledgment of the equality upon which they are so insistent. But unless this acknowledgment could also be expected to yield tangible consequences in the Persian Gulf, it would represent in the end little more than an empty gesture. Is there any plausible reason for believing that the Soviets would have been satisfied by such a gesture, or that they might be so satisfied today?

It is the prospect of a very difficult and dangerous relationship with the Soviet Union that is the principal objection to a policy whose first priority is the restoration of American power generally and, above all, in the Persian Gulf. Yet unless one argues that such restoration is simply unnecessary there is no alternative to it. The risks it gives rise to can only be weighed against those that must be run through failing to respond to a still growing Soviet strategic and conventional arms momentum.

This momentum, moreover, cannot be broken on the level of strategic arms by the acceptance of SALT II or a modified version of the agreement. The momentum SALT II would halt is principally of a quantitative character and relates to weapons that the Soviet Union has no compelling incentive to multiply even in the absence of agreement. The fear that without an agreement the Soviets would embark on a huge expansion of their present strategic forces is in all likelihood groundless. Instead, the expectation must be that they will concentrate their future efforts in areas that fall largely outside the purview of SALT II, whether these are qualitative improvements of existing weapons systems or the development of altogether new systems. Whatever the merits of the strategic arms limitation agreement, they are not to be found in the brake they are alleged to impose on a still growing Soviet arms momentum.

3

If the risks inherent in the Soviet-American relationship cannot be exorcised by the simple refusal to acknowledge their existence, is there nevertheless substantial reason to believe they can be kept to a moderate threshold? While pursuing a restoration of American power and position, and while once again drawing lines that the Soviets are not expected to violate, can we still keep the relationship short of one that is under constant strain? Is it plausible to expect a U.S. policy that will involve, in the phrase of Robert Legvold, "containment without confrontation"?*

This would be a far more attractive prospect than the one indicated in these pages. What would a U.S. policy toward the Soviet Union look like that might be expected to lead to this happier relationship? Legvold argues that it

> must proceed on two tracks: one of firmness, military strength (but not by seeking military superiority), and a will to act (requiring a public readier for the possibility); the other of cooperation, the extended hand, and a renewed interest in dealing with problems jointly rather than in turning problems against each other.†

---

*Robert Legvold, "Containment Without Confrontation," *Foreign Policy* (Fall 1980), pp. 74–98.

†Legvold,, "Containment Without Confrontation," p. 93.

The first track would provide the means of a refurbished policy of containment and draw the lines of such policy. The second track would provide the incentive for the Soviet Union to accept, though perhaps not without occasional lapses, the first. It would include "an economic policy founded on cooperation," "arms control efforts as a significant and carefully coordinated element in a national security policy that does not rely only on arming," and "a serious attempt to open the one area of detente that never got started, namely crisis management."*

This is clearly a prescription for a return to the policy of the early 1970s, though a return without the illusions of these earlier years. Legvold's "sound, resurrected detente" is a detente that is based on power and a willingness to use that power. It does not assume that Moscow will refrain from seeking "marginal advantages" in the Third World, but rather accepts that Moscow will be so tempted and that the temptation must be countered by a combintaion of threats, rewards, and a growing recognition—encouraged by institutionalized procedures—of mutuality of interest in managing the inevitable competition. The earlier detente presumably failed because it was too soft where it should have been harder and too hard where it should have been softer. A resurrected detente can proceed on the basis of this experience and can do so without having to contend with the domestic constraints of the early to mid-1970s.

---

*Legvold, "Containment Without Confrontation," p. 95.

Is it reasonable to believe that Legvold's detente would enjoy a better fate than its predecessor? One must doubt that it would. This is so even if we freely grant the assumption that this detente would not suffer from the domestic constraints attending the implementation of the earlier detente. The principal question the Nixon-Kissinger policy raised — What would induce the Soviet Union to become more moderate and no longer seek to exploit opportunities and take advantage of instabilities? — must also be raised by current proposals for a resurrected detente. Moreover, this question must be raised in circumstances much less auspicious than those of an earlier period.

Whereas the detente of 1972 was undertaken at a time when this country still enjoyed a position of net superiority in the arms balance, this no longer holds. And whereas the detente of 1972 was undertaken at a time when the temptations held out by the Third World appeared to have receded, today they have sharply risen — especially in the most critical area of the Third World. Finally, Soviet insistence upon being treated as an equal of America, with all that this implies in the various areas of competition, has markedly increased. The time when Moscow could be appeased or fobbed off with the symbols of equality has passed.

Against these considerations, what are the incentives that might induce Moscow to accept an American-inspired definition of moderate behavior? We speak of incentives, not disincentives or threats. The latter are synonymous with the old methods of containment. They are quite compatible with and even presuppose occasional confrontation. The promise of detente is to avoid confrontation, though not at the price of steady sacrifice of interest. But can a new detente be more successful at preventing this than the old detente?

The belief that a more cooperative economic policy might do so is surely a slender reed to rely on. Those who continue to do so have yet to demonstrate how such a policy, once free of the Jackson-Vanik Amendment and other impediments, could promote more than a modest relationship without creating more economic risks than benefits for the United States. They would also have to indicate the benefits—whether in trade, credit facilities, or technology transfers—that the Soviets do not already enjoy in increasing measure by virtue of their economic relationship with West European countries. Even if these propositions could be persuasively demonstrated, they would still have to indicate why the Soviet Union might be expected to do what it has never done before: subordinate high policy to such benefits as an improved economic relationship might bring. In this regard, it may be recalled that the first serious test (and failure) of the promise of detente, the 1973 Arab-Israeli war, preceded the Jackson-Vanik Amendment.

The emphasis placed by advocates of a new detente on a continuing and even greater effort toward arms control is easy to understand though difficult to credit. It is easy to understand since the SALT process has come to be seen as the principal achievement of the old detente. In the course of the 1970s, this process was increasingly viewed as constituting the principal ongoing method of political communication with the Soviet Union, the jeopardizing of which would enhance the prospects of nuclear war. Not surprisingly, this view became the more insistent as the normal forms of communication atrophied in the wake of Afghanistan.

Yet the emphasis placed on the SALT process remains difficult to credit. In the last eight years SALT has not hindered the Soviets from pursuing substantially the same arms buildup we have every reason to believe they would have pursued in its absence. Nor did it prevent Moscow from exploiting situations in the Third World. We have no way of knowing what the Soviet Union might have done in the Third World without SALT. But it is special pleading to point to Afghanistan as an example of what might have occurred earlier had it not been for Soviet interest in arms control. There are many reasons that account for Afghanistan. The Soviet calculation in late 1979 that the cause of SALT II had been lost — at least for the time being — could only have been one such reason and likely a subordinate one.

If we put aside economic policy and arms control, there remains the area of crisis management, of dealing jointly with problems arising from superpower competition in the Third World. Without question, this has been, as Legvold and others remind us, the area in which the old detente never got started. It is also the area that more than any other proved fatal to the old detente. The reasons it did so, however, must surely tell us something about the prospects held out by a new detente, for these reasons are clearly no less relevant today than they were in the early to mid-1970s.

If the Soviet leadership was unwilling then to acquiesce in a definition of equality that, in its eyes, denied Moscow the substance of equality, it is all the more unwilling to do so today. An improved military position has given added weight to Soviet insistence upon equal rights in the Third World. The rising opportunities for exploiting instabilities have made the claim almost compelling in its attraction. On the American side, though the arms balance has steadily moved in an adverse direction, there is an increasing disposition to resist Moscow's claim to equal rights. This is so not only because of a general change in the climate of opinion—a change resulting in part from the experience with the old detente —but also, and more important, because of the rising fear that the claim, once acknowledged in principle, would soon be applied to regions of critical interest to this country.

In these circumstances, the prospects for crisis management must be rated as very low. Nor is it apparent why in these circumstances crisis management is intrinsically desirable, even if presently unobtainable. Clearly, it is desirable if such management may operate within a framework of state relations to which the parties can meaningfully subscribe. Within this framework, the competition of the great powers for position and advantage has been difficult enough to manage. Without it, the search for crisis management — in effect, for mutually agreed upon "rules of the game" — must either prove barren or lead to undesirable results. The search itself necessarily presumes the basis for the desired goal, or else the effort to fashion reliable patterns of contraint must prove feckless. Unfortunately, the evidence that this basis exists is no more convincing today than it was in the period of the cold war.

4

The renewed search for detente with the Soviet Union, a detente without the illusions and excessive expectations attending the old detente, reflects the fear that in its absence we will be tempted to return to something akin to the policy of containment that prevailed from the early 1950s to the mid-1960s. In turn, that fear finds a twofold expression. In one, if we attempt to resurrect the containment of yesterday in the conditions of today, we may well tempt the Soviets to exploit their present position of strength in a manner that will lead to an ultimate confrontation. In the other, if we attempt and even partially succeed in resurrecting the containment of yesterday, we will tempt ourselves to repeat the excesses of yesterday. Thus, whether we fail or succeed, the alternatives to a new detente are seen as forbidding.

There is no need, however, to accept a policy of global containment as the only alternative to a new detente. The

Soviet-American relationship may take yet other expressions and hold out less forbidding consequences, even in the short term. What American policy cannot avoid, save at the risk of sacrificing its international position and gravely jeopardizing its security, are the measures outlined earlier in this essay. But these measures form no more than a limited policy of containment. They respond essentially to the same security interests that an earlier policy of containment responded to in the years immediately following World War II. Even so, a policy of moderate containment today would necessarily differ from the moderate containment of the late 1940s because we cannot regain the relative power advantage we once enjoyed. Certainly there is no way we can recapture the immunity from direct attack we once enjoyed; nor can we determine the behavior of our principal allies in the manner we once could.

These changes, not to speak of the changes that have occurred in the once passive Third World, require us to recognize that we could pursue the methods and the aspirations that characterized an earlier period of containment only at very great cost and effort, and even then with no more than a modest prospect of success. If this is so, the containment of today and tomorrow will have to deal with the Soviet Union in a manner that those who presided over containment in the past were often reluctant to accept. This containment will have to make concessions and compromises in areas of contention where concession and compromise were once spurned. If it is at all prudent, a refurbished containment will avoid measures that sharply exacerbate the relationship with the Soviet Union and make the prospect of its future amelioration virtually impossible.

Nothing would be more likely to have these effects than a military alliance, even if only de facto, with China. Yet this is the direction in which American policy was inexorably moving in the last year of the Carter Administration. If it had carried forward much more, whatever the ostensible justification given for doing so, it would have sealed the Soviet-American relationship in a fixed and truly dangerous mold by making it hostage to our relations with China. It would not have mattered that this was done from a position of growing strength rather than one of relative weakness.

The promise of a policy of limited containment envisaged here is not the promise of detente or even of a "sound, resurrected detente." It suggests competition far more than cooperation. It finds the sources of this competition primarily in the structural causes of conflict between the superpowers rather than in the still profoundly different visions of the world and of the state system that the two entertain.

Even so, the great ideological divide that continues to separate the Soviet Union and the United States remains an important source of conflict. When combined with the structural causes, the result gives the Soviet-American relationship greater continuity with the past than is commonly acknowledged. It is this continuity in change that prompts some to insist that a policy of limited or selective containment will not work, and that the logic of our position requires a resurgent America in pursuit of goals reminiscent of the later period of containment.

It is also this continuity in change that makes it apparent, when examining the debate over containment today, that we are destined to retrace an old argument. In many respects our current alternatives are strikingly similar to the alternatives held out in the years that followed World War II. The two principal versions of containment that vied with one another then promise to become major sources of contention today.

5

The case for pursuing a policy of global containment is essentially the same today as it was in the period that preceded Vietnam. It does not rest upon a denial of the changes that have occurred in the intervening period. Those who urge that we have no real alternative but to revert to the policy that was abandoned in the late 1960s are not oblivious to the changes of a decade and more. They may and do believe that many of these changes are not to be considered as historical "givens" to which we must henceforth adjust our behavior. Clearly, they believe that with the requisite will and effort, much that we came to accept in the 1970s as virtually unalterable can be altered to our advantage. But this assessment of the nature of the change that has occurred is not to be confused with the denial of change itself. If anything, the view considered here is distinctive in its insistence upon the momentous transformation that has taken place since the 1960s, and above all in the relationship of the superpowers.

At the same time, the result of change does not invalidate the essential rationale of, and need for a return to, the policy of global containment. Until we have made substantial progress toward redressing the arms balance with the Soviet Union, containment will have to be conducted with considerable prudence and circumspection. Even so, the argument runs, the critical assumptions that formed the basis of containment in the pre-Vietnam period remain as valid today as they were then. Indeed, in some respects they appear more compelling than ever.

It is the military power now at the disposal of the Soviet Union, and the apparent determination of Soviet leaders to employ this power to expansionist ends, that prompts this conclusion. The persisting controversy and residual uncertainty over Soviet motivation, whether in general or in any particular case, does not matter a great deal. Even if the assumption of some observers is granted and Soviet expansion is found to arise primarily from a deep and pervasive geopolitical insecurity, the issue would remain how this insecurity might be satisfied short of jeopardizing the vital security interests of others. In terms of objective consequences, there may be little to choose between expansion motivated by geopolitical insecurity and expansion that provides its own motivation.

These considerations are in any event deemed insufficient to the degree that they ignore the distinctive nature of the Soviet regime. The insecurity of Soviet rulers is not simply a function of an experience that is, after all, scarcely unique in the history of continental powers. It is as much, if not far more, a function of the manner in which the world beyond Moscow's control is viewed by a regime that has always postulated an adversarial relationship with this world, if for no other reason than that the legitimacy of the Soviet regime has depended in significant measure upon laying claim to such relationship. The intensity with which this hostility is expressed has varied. It cannot be abandoned, however, as long as the "mellowing of Soviet power" George Kennan speculated about some 34 years ago has not taken place.*

Although the Soviet Union of today is not the Soviet

---

*George F. Kennan, "The Sources of Soviet Conduct," *Foreign Affairs* (July 1947), p. 582. The passage from which the above phrase is taken reads: "It would be an exaggeration to say that American behavior unassisted and alone could exercise a power of life and death over the Communist movement and bring about the early fall of Soviet power in Russia. But the United States has it in its power to increase enormously the strains under which Soviet policy must operate, to force upon the Kremlin a far greater degree of moderation and circumspection than it has had to observe in recent years, and in this way to promote tendencies which must eventually find their outlet in either the break-up or the gradual mellowing of Soviet power." The author of these words concluded a number of years ago that a very considerable mellowing of Soviet power had since taken place and that Soviet leaders were not more motivated by a sense of external insecurity than by inner insecurity — that is, the obsessive search for legitimacy.

Union of the years following World War II, it is just as clearly not a state that has broken from the basic pattern of totalitarian rule. The need to secure the legitimacy of the regime may not press upon its present rulers to the same degree that this need haunted their predecessors. Still, the need remains despite the longevity of the system and the measures taken in the post-Stalin period to broaden the base of the elites who have a stake in the maintenance of the system. That need continues to find expression in the deep-rooted suspicion of and hostility toward the West the Soviet regime has manifested since its inception.

Thus the issue that has always placed the Soviet Union at odds with the West persists. Not surprisingly, the policy of detente had no substantial effect on this issue, despite the illusions entertained at the time that it would. If anything, detente could be expected to make Soviet leaders more sensitive to the matter of the regime's legitimacy and to the manner in which the peoples of the Soviet Union and of Eastern Europe, by contrast to the nations of the West, are governed. Even a modestly improved relationship with the West must invite comparisons and give rise to expectations that could be permitted to find expression only at the risk of threatening political stability.

Nor is the case for global containment found to be affected by the consideration that the ideological appeal the Soviet regime once enjoyed in much of the world and was able to use to advantage is now almost completely spent. Without question, the "curiosity" that Kennan remarked on at the outset of the cold war—"that the ideological power of Soviet authority is strongest today in areas beyond the frontiers of Russia, beyond the reach of its police power"*—is today scarcely more than an historical relic, the victim of forces of nationalism and independence Moscow has been either unable to control or able to do so only by the use of military power. Yet the loss of one form of power has been more than compensated by the gain of another. What the Soviet Union has suffered in the loss of an attractive ideology has been recouped by a growing military capability that can be deployed in areas that were once beyond Moscow's effective reach. A world that is ever more determinedly pluralistic provides no assurance that this capability will not be effectively employed, even if it does impose severe limits on the use that an expansionist regime may make of an ideology having universalist pretensions. But the triumph of nationalism affords no guarantee against expansion undertaken either directly by force or indirectly by the military support of regimes that, however nationalistic their aspirations, are ready to make a pact with the devil to see those aspirations realized.

To its advocates, then, the case for global containment is not weakened by what appears today as a conflict in which conventional forms of power have become more

---

*Kennan, "The Sources of Soviet Conduct," p. 580.

prominent. Even if it is granted that the ideological salience of the conflict between the superpowers has declined, the more conventional aspects of the struggle have not. The latter impose a familiar logic that can be resisted only by placing oneself in a position of serious disadvantage, a position we persisted in taking during the past decade. We did so by neglecting — and in some instances even disavowing — the necessities imposed by the conflict whose essential nature and dynamic have remained unchanged since the years following World War II.

The results of the various rationalizations given for this desire to escape from a world dominated by a pervasive rivalry between the United States and the Soviet Union — whether such rationalization took the form of insisting that a bipolar world had been succeeded by a pentagonal world, or that the previous contest had been transformed by its marked amelioration (detente), or that the superpowers could in any event no longer pursue their conflict by traditional means given the radical decline in the utility of military power, or that a new division of the world (North-South) had largely taken the place of the old (East-West) — are now apparent for all to see. The conflict over which so much ingenuity and effort were devoted in order either to deny its reality altogether or to transform its character has reasserted itself with a vengeance. It has done so in circumstances that have placed us at a marked and dangerous disadvantage.

Although the results of a misspent decade are now increasingly recognized, there remains an unwillingness to accept the consequences that follow from the logic of the competition. That logic has never permitted, and does not permit today, the kind of selectivity in containing Soviet expansion that many persist in believing possible. From the outset of containment in the 1940s, the attempt to distinguish which areas are vital to American security has generally floundered when put to a practical test.* The significance of an area cannot be detetermined in the abstract; it must be considered in the full context of the circumstances attending a decision whether or not to protect it. In the abstract, the judgment reached in the late 1940s that Korea should be considered a marginal interest, and accordingly placed outside the American defense perimeter in Asia, may have appeared quite reasonable. In the circumstances of June 1950, it did not. In the abstract the Soviet attack upon Afghanistan in 1979 might have been seen as an occasion that scarcely called

---

*It is useful to recall that at this earlier time the man whom many have seen in retrospect as the leading advocate of selective containment, George Kennan, supported aid to Greece and Turkey (1947), advocated interventionary measures to forestall or counter the threat posed by a communist victory in the Italian elections (1948), and agreed with the decision to intervene in Korea (1950). He did so, among other reasons, because he acknowledged the psychological effect that communist victories in these countries might have elsewhere. Though they were not themselves areas of vital interest in Kennan's estimation, their fate could affect areas he considered to be of vital interest.

for a strong American reaction. Yet in the context of the events that marked the Soviet action, a very different conclusion appeared warranted.

In both of these cases the difficulties of selective containment are presumably illuminated. Taken in isolation, the argument that South Korea was an interest of little intrinsic value seemed plausible and even persuasive. But South Korea could not be considered in isolation. Instead, an American failure to respond in Korea had to be considered in terms of the effects this failure might have elsewhere, above all in Europe where the fear of Soviet attack was pervasive. Even if that fear was misplaced, its importance was such that it could not be ignored. Moreover, who can say what conclusions Soviet leaders might have drawn had the United States not responded as it did to the attack on South Korea?

Again, taken in isolation, the Soviet invasion of Afghanistan might be seen as posing no serious threat to vital Western interests. A state comprising a part of the Soviet borderlands, and one that Moscow had for several years asserted increasing control over while the Western powers registered little opposition, suddenly threatened to break from the Soviet hold. In reasserting their control, by whatever brutal means, the Soviets simply sought to keep what they were already conceded to have. Yet the Soviet action provoked an American reaction that, in its long-term consequences, may well prove to be of momentous significance. The armed intervention in Afghanistan could not be considered in isolation; it illuminated the sea change that had occurred during the past decade in the military relationship of the superpowers. Coming as it did in the wake of the Iranian revolution and the seizure of American embassy officials, it emphasized with dramatic effect the extent of Western vulnerability in the Gulf region.

Even if the Soviet move into Afghanistan was initially motivated solely by the desire to protect a sphere of influence that had already been conceded to it, there was no way of calculating the psychological effects of American inaction on the states of the region. Nor was there any way of knowing what conclusions Soviet leaders might draw about their prospects in the Gulf in the absence of an American response. Indeed, to many it has been the utter inadequacy of that response — an inadequacy measured by the failure to contest the Soviet move by supplying substantial military aid to the Afghan resistance — that has served to weaken further the perception of American power among those who had already begun to discount it.

The moral drawn from these and other examples by the proponents of global containment is clear: lines cannot be drawn, even as a matter of general principle. So long as world politics continues to be dominated by a bipolar power structure, and so long as the competition between the two superpowers retains the same basic features it has exhibited since the outset of the post–World War II period, we cannot pick and choose those places where we must contain Soviet expansion. When engaged in a conflict for global stakes, what may appear as a marginal interest will be invested with a significance it would not otherwise have, for almost any challenge is likely to be seen by the challenger and by third parties as a test of one's will.

The familiar process at work here was long ago articulated by Thucydides in explaining why Athens risked war with Sparta rather than accept an otherwise apparently moderate demand of its great rival. "Let none of you think," Pericles says in urging his fellow Athenians to reject Sparta's demand,

> that we should be going to war for a trifle if we refuse to revoke the Megarian decree. It is a point they make much of, and say that war need not take place if we revoke this decree; but, if we do go to war, let there be no kind of suspicion in your hearts that the war is over a small matter. For you this trifle is both the assurance and the proof of your determination. If you give in, you will immediately be confronted with some greater demand, since they will think that you only gave way on this point through fear.*

The message of Thucydides is that in a great conflict even apparently marginal interests can be of crucial significance in terms of their effects on core interests. It is in such conflicts, characterized by their pervasiveness and seeming intractability, that discrete issues will not and cannot be viewed in isolation. The logic, or the psychologic, of the conflict inevitably creates a relationship of

---

*Thucydides, *History of the Peloponnesian War*, trans. Rex Warner (London: Penguin Books, 1954), p. 92.

noncore to core interests. Both the ultimate stakes and the inner dynamic of the conflict prevent making a clear distinction between what may otherwise be seen as marginal and central. In the end, the periphery has a way of becoming the center if challenges to it are not dealt with effectively.

This argument has a familiar ring, for it is essentially the same argument that was employed to defend our commitment in Vietnam. The proponents of a return to global containment do not shrink from acknowledging the affinity. Their response is that Vietnam should not have been seen and should not be seen today as discrediting the policy that led to American involvement in the war. Instead, Vietnam should be regarded as an unfortunate application of an otherwise sound and desirable policy. Whether the misfortune consisted in the decision to intervene in circumstances as unpromising as Vietnam or rather in the manner by which the intervention, once made, was implemented, the experience of the war is in no way found to have invalidated the premises on which global containment rested. These premises remain as sound as ever, though the dramatic growth in Soviet military power has made acting on them more demanding and hazardous than ever.

6

If, according to its advocates, the need for global containment is at least as great today as it was in the past, the question persists whether this policy can be restored in the absence of the motivations that once gave rise to it. Is it enough to point to the growth in Soviet military power and to the dangers this growth and the aspirations attending it hold out? Here again, the experience of Vietnam is found instructive. Although the effect of the war discredited containment in general, it discredited above all the ideological roots of containment. In their place was substituted the realpolitik considerations we have come to associate with the Nixon-Kissinger policy reformulation.

Yet in doing so, it is argued, the distinctive character of Soviet-American rivalry was obscured, with the result that it became increasingly difficult to sustain the more modest policy that emerged in the early 1970s. The detente of 1972 appeared to complete the process of virtually emptying the competition between the Soviet Union and the United States of ideological content. If the message of detente was not that the competition as such had ended, it was clearly that the contest was henceforth expected to take a more conventional form. The idiom of the Nixon-Kissinger policy reformulation reflected this expectation, for it was on the whole the familiar language of traditional statecraft rather than that characterizing the earlier years of the cold war.

The failure of that policy, it is contended, cannot be separated from the rationale on which its architects sought to base it. Though the "new structure of peace" required continued effort if America's position and in-

147

terests in the world were to be preserved, the willingness to make this effort was not forthcoming largely because the public did not respond and could not be made to respond to a foreign policy that appeared to have no greater appeal than to national self-interest. In abandoning the ideological dimension of Soviet-American rivalry, the will to defend even core interests began to erode. That erosion was checked only when the force of self-interest became so apparent and compelling that it could no longer be ignored. Even so, without fully acknowledging once again the ideological dimension of the rivalry, we may well fail to mount the effort necessary to protect interests clearly synonymous with our core security.

The case for recognizing the continuing importance — indeed, the central importance — of the element of the conflict that became unfashionable to mention in the 1970s has been most forcefully and acutely made by Norman Podhoretz.* It is not sufficient, Podhoretz has argued, to treat the Soviet-American rivalry in the manner of conventional great power contests. But, the "new nationalism" that has arisen in reaction to the visible decline of American power has the tendency to do just that. Though itself a needed and healthy reaction to the passivity and defeatism of the 1970s, Podhoretz finds in this reaction little awareness of the deeper meaning of the conflict. Yet without giving a deeper meaning to Soviet-

---

*Norman Podhoretz, *The Present Danger* (New York: Simon & Schuster, 1980).

American rivalry, now more serious in its possible implications than it has ever been, he fears that the requisite
base for carrying us into and sustaining a new period of
containment will prove lacking. The term that is still
missing from a long overdue reaction to a policy of
strategic retreat is communism. Without that term, and
an awareness of all that it implies, the change we are
witnessing today will lack direction and purpose. Podhoretz writes

> In resisting the advance of Soviet power we *are* fighting for
> freedom and against Communism, for democracy and
> against totalitarianism. Yet it is precisely this sense of things
> that the new nationalism thus far lacks. . . . Without such
> clarity, the new nationalism is unlikely to do more than lead
> to sporadic outbursts of indignant energy.*

It is in Podhoretz's outlook that we may find perhaps
the clearest advocacy of a resurgent America committed
again to the goals of a policy of global containment.
Although directed in the first instance against Soviet expansion, it is not and indeed cannot be limited to this
end. A relative indifference to the coming to power of
communist governments generally, so long as these governments maintained a position of substantial independence from Moscow, would of necessity carry the implica-
tion that opposition to Soviet expansion was based more
on traditional grounds of realpolitik than on ideology. It
would suggest that opposition to Soviet expansion is

---

*Podhoretz, *The Present Danger,* pp. 100–1.

rooted more in the customary consequences great power expansion has entailed than in the particular consequences that Soviet expansion is found to entail. But this would tend to reduce Soviet-American competition to a conventional great power contest. In turn, the "deeper meaning" of the contest would be obscured or lost and the requisite base for mounting the effort to resist the advance of Soviet power would be jeopardized.*

Given these considerations, opposition to the coming to power of communist governments cannot be based simply on the relationship they may or may not be expected to have with the Soviet Union. To be sure, the expectation that the relationship will be intimate, and particularly that it will have a military dimension, affords an additional strong reason for a policy designed to oppose the advent of communist regimes. Even in the absence of such expectation, however, opposition to the emergence of such regimes must form a prime desideratum of policy, to be tempered only by the constraints of prudence. The ideological claim cannot be compromised, let alone abandoned, before the "fact" — assuming it to be such — of pluralism. Today, as yesterday, the meaning of a policy

---

*Podhoretz has subsequently underlined these considerations in his essay, "The Future Danger," *Commentary* (April 1981), pp. 29–47. The future danger, he writes, is "that a strategy of containment which defines the problem as Soviet expansionism alone will be unable to sustain the requisite political support and will therefore lead almost as surely as the retrenchments of the Carter era to [a] Soviet-dominated world."

of global containment must be synonymous with opposition to the expansion of communism.

7

While the Podhoretz argument does not establish either the need for or the desirability of global containment today, it does underscore a critical feature of the American experience in foreign policy. No activist foreign policy in this century has been sustained simply by the appeal to conventional security interests. Instead, a broader rationale has always been necessary to elicit the support required to preserve interests on which even the nation's core security has depended.

In abandoning isolationism in the 1930s, we not only responded to a perceived threat to our physical and economic security, but we also recoiled from the prospect of a world in which America's political and economic frontiers would become coterminous with its territorial frontiers, a world in which societies that shared our institutions and values might very possibly disappear — in sum, a world in which the American example and American influence would become irrelevant. In such a world, it was argued, America could no longer realize its promise since a hostile world from which America was shut out would inevitably affect the integrity of the nation's institutions and the quality of its domestic life. The issues of physical security and economic well-being apart, it was to prevent this prospect from materializing that the nation abandoned its interwar isolationism, intervened in World War II, and, in the years following the war, adopted a policy of containment. It has been to prevent this same prospect that we have been willing to incur the risk of physical destruction through nuclear war, rather than abandon interests that would not jeopardize our physical existence if once lost.

This experience indicates that the initial and indispensable stimulus prompting the exercise of American power has been a perceived threat to the nation's physical security or material well-being. It also points to the inadequacy of conventional security calculations in sustaining the exercise of American power. Once the initial threat has brought forth a response, America has needed a broader rationale for the effort and sacrifice required to sustain the exercise of power. When it has not been forthcoming or when it has been discredited, the result has been drift and uncertainty. So it was that in the early stages of containment the response that was initially evoked, largely as a result of conventional security considerations, was sustained and even expanded by what came to be a still broader motive for policy. When that broader motive was discredited, as it was by Vietnam, even the narrower and conventional security policy became difficult to sustain.

This experience is found to support the view that our alternatives today are either a return to the policy that was abandoned in the late 1960s or a policy that will prove inadequate to sustain the power and discipline to protect interests on which our core security depends. Yet what the American experience appears to bear out is simply the need for a broader rationale than that afforded by the appeal to physical and economic security. If so, there is no apparent reason for insisting that this need can be satisfied only by a policy of global containment, since moderate or selective containment also has a rationale that transcends narrow self-interest. It has a broader rationale today just as it had a broader rationale in the period when containment began.

The debate that attended the early years of containment was not one between those who had little, if any, concern beyond the immediate needs of American security and those who did. Though the earlier debate ultimately turned on two different views of the requirements of American security, it is important not to exaggerate the differences between them. The circumstances of the late 1940s made the application of containment roughly identical with a balance-of-power policy. Yet even then, containment in Europe was from the outset undertaken for reasons that went beyond security, narrowly construed. Here, as well as in the case of Japan, the intent was not only to prevent these centers of industrial power from falling under Soviet control, but also to insure that they would remain — or become — democratic societies. From the outset, the policy of moderate containment expressed a security interest that went beyond a conventional security interest in balance-of-power terms to identify security with the internal order maintained by states. Though modest, it still implied a scheme of things that went beyond the order implicit in a balance of power. This scheme cannot be equated with the universalist pretensions of the Truman Doctrine; it also cannot be equated with a narrow and traditional conception of security.

The differences between the two initial views of containment were relative, not absolute. Had this not been the case, it would have been much more difficult than it was to move from the narrower and more conventional view of security characteristics of the early years of containment to the broader view that came to prevail in the period following Korea. Still, these relative differences were important. They carried distinctive implications not only about the kind of world we needed for our security, but also about the kind of world we wanted. In both cases it was very difficult to distinguish need from want.

At the same time, this apparent inability to separate the two was far more pronounced in the policy of global containment that ultimately came to prevail, and that found a near perfect expression in its first real test: Vietnam. It was need that presumably dictated our intervention in Vietnam. For those who had grasped the deeper meaning of America's postwar policy, the familiar question posed by administration officials in the mid-1960s — Why are we in Vietnam? — could be no more than rhetorical. The great issue raised by Vietnam was how the international system was to be organized and maintained. Was this system to be one of consent or one of coercion, one that safeguarded the right of peoples to choose their

own destiny or one that destroyed this right, one that provided an environment favorable to the growth of free institutions or one that encouraged the spread of arbitrary
power?

This was the ultimate issue that the Kennedy and
Johnson Administrations found at stake in Vietnam, and
it involved nothing less than the equation of world order
and American security. If the people of South Vietnam
were not to be permitted to determine their own destiny
in their own way, the foundations of the world order we
had sought to establish and to maintain since World War
II would be imperiled. If this order were thus imperiled,
America's security would also be placed in jeopardy. Accordingly, we were in South Vietnam for both the South
Vietnamese and for ourselves.

There was no novelty in this essential rationale given
for the war. The same theme, with the same fusion of arguments, formed the substance of the first statement of
global containment in 1947. Instead, the difference between the Truman Doctrine and the Johnson Administration's defense of Vietnam was to be found in the
notable lack of success the Johnson Administration enjoyed in making this rationale persuasive to many who
had previously supported American foreign policy. The
dilemma of the Johnson Administration was its inability
to successfully represent the war in Vietnam either as a
vindication of the principles of freedom and self-determination or as a measure indispensable for American
security. Without question, the growing opposition to

the war was a reflection of its mounting costs and seemingly inconclusive results. Yet it was also in large measure a reflection of the growing conviction that the war was not a response to need and that it had been entered into for reasons that could not justify the sacrifices entailed.

It is ironic that although Vietnam led to the discrediting of containment—surely to its more expansive version and, in some measure, to its narrower version—it did not lead to the rejection of the aspirations that had been so important in prompting the intervention. We had been led to Vietnam largely by virtue of the promise of a world that was expected to move progressively under American leadership toward the eventual triumph of liberal-capitalist values. In accepting defeat in Vietnam—even more, in rejecting a policy of global containment—this promise presumably would have to be abandoned. At no time, however, did we reconcile ourselves to the prospect of a world in which a large, and perhaps increasing, part outside the industrial democracies would resist American influence.

If that prospect is viewed with renewed concern today, it is not so viewed only by the proponents of a resurgent America. Even those who decry the call for a resurgent America and insistently remind us that we no longer have the power to shape the world according to our desires appear uneasy over accepting the prospect of a world in which American influence would decline. The officials of the Carter Administration, including the president, were no doubt quite sincere in expressing the desire to see the developing world move in a manner that would ultimately prove congenial to us. To be sure, they advocated the need for America "to get on the side of change." But they did so in order to guide and to manage the great changes they found sweeping the world. Through different and more congenial methods than those that were often employed in the past, they nonetheless aspired to achieve the goals of the past.

This strategy inevitably failed. The goals of the past could not be achieved while foreswearing the methods that once attended those goals. Nor can a policy of moderate containment escape incurring the risk of intervention. Clearly, it cannot do so in the Persian Gulf. Circumstances there may prove even more ambiguous than those attending past interventions. It will not do to charge that a resurgent America will be an interventionist America. Any policy of containment must accept the risk of intervention, and in circumstances that we may find in many ways undesirable.

8

Still, there are risks and risks, just as there are interventions and interventions. It would be disingenuous to deny that the risks and costs likely to attend a return to the former policy of global containment would be anything less than considerable. Nor can these risks be disposed of by assuming that the global containment of the future will differ from the containment of the past in that it will be characterized by greater prudence, by greater care in discriminating between interests, and by greater readiness to accept the prospect of periodic defeat. If this assumption is once granted there may be very little to choose from between global and limited containment. The outlook of the one becomes in practice almost indistinguishable from the outlook of the other.

It is true that in principle there may still appear to be a substantial difference between the two. Even in principle, however, the difference may be reduced to marginal proportions. If global containment no longer finds a "seamless web of interests" in the conflict, while moderate or limited containment acknowledges that even otherwise marginal interests can prove crucial in their effects on core interests, one heretofore important difference in principle must markedly recede in significance.

The same may be said of the varying emphasis placed on the ideological features of the conflict. Anticommunism may provide, as it has in the past, the motor force for global containment. Even so, a very different treatment may be accorded, as it has occasionally been accorded in the past, to communist regimes that are clearly independent of the Soviet Union. Moderate containment, on the other hand, cannot be and is not indifferent to the ideological ties that bind us to the industrial democracies. Moreover, it cannot be and generally has not been indifferent to the nature of the relationship between the Soviet Union and emergent communist regimes. Particularly where that relationship takes a military expression, the policy consequences drawn may well be coincidental with the policy consequences drawn by global containment.

In this manner, the differences between the two containments are made to appear almost inconsequential. A "mature" global containment seems little more than a moderate or selective containment whose horizons have been properly broadened. Yet the differences between the two containments cannot be so readily bridged for they are rooted in quite divergent views of the world and of the American role in it. Thus moderate containment, as its critics have regularly noted, has nearly always reflected a view of the world that remains more a promise than a reality. Resistant as it is to the constraints imposed by a bipolar system, its tendency is to exaggerate the opportunities held out by pluralism. These opportunities, if only properly exploited, are expected to provide the great deliverance from the hardships and dangers of global containment. At the same time, these same opportunities are expected to enable us to identify with, and even to guide, the great changes taking place in the developing world.

If these are the characteristic illusions of moderate containment, they are no greater than the illusions commonly nourished by supporters of global containment. The latter may have few illusions about the persistent reality of bipolarity and the constraints it imposes, but they have little disposition to acknowledge the consequences to which global containment must lead. This reluctance may be seen in the manner in which our Vietnam experience is treated. But Vietnam cannot be properly seen as an aberration of global containment. It was not simply an unfortunate misapplication of a policy whose outlook and objectives must normally be expected to lead to very different results. The meaning of Vietnam is not that we chose a very poor place to wage a war, though this we surely did. Nor can the meaning of Vietnam be found in the methods by which we chose to wage the war, though these methods surely were wanting.

These and other explanations undoubtedly express limited truths about the war. Yet they do not express the most important truth about Vietnam, which must be found in the policy and outlook that made not intervention as such but this particular kind of intervention — one that the nation could never really understand and, when its costs became clear, would not support — an ever present possibility. Vietnam was not, as many critics would have it, the perfect embodiment of global containment; it was an outcome that was always implicit in this policy. Even more, it was an outcome that sooner or later was inevitable.

To explain Vietnam as a mistake in the sense that "the interests at stake in Southeast Asia were simply not vital enough to justify the risk,"* is to apply a calculus that was quite alien to the policy that led to our intervention. It is to apply the calculus of moderate or selective containment to the policy of global containment. To be sure, global containment had its calculus, but it was not of the kind that lent itself to the manner of judgment reached above. At the time, those who justified the intervention did not rest their case simply on the interests at stake in Southeast Asia. Had they done so, they might well have reached a very different conclusion from the one they did.

As true believers in global containment, however, they would not and could not do so. Vietnam could not be seen only in terms of its intrinsic significance or, for that matter, even in terms of Southeast Asia. Instead, it had to be seen in relation to the greater interests that were presumably at stake in the war, interests that transcended Vietnam and Southeast Asia. Ultimately, the Johnson Administration equated its commitment in Vietnam with its commitments elsewhere. The integrity of the latter was made to depend upon the integrity of the former. Even if it were conceded, the argument ran, that the initial commitment in South Vietnam was unwise, the relevant consideration was that the commitment had been made. This being so, there remained no alternative but

*Podhoretz, *The Present Danger,* p. 28. This was at the time the judgment of Hans Morgenthau, and Podhoretz considers it in retrospect as "sound, and even irrefutable."

to honor it. If we failed to honor it, the administration of the day insisted, all else would once again be placed in doubt. Thus the global structure of American interests and commitments was considered to depend on the outcome of the war.

This was the logic that prompted the intervention in Vietnam and led to an ever deeper involvement once the initial commitment had been made. Moreover, the argument became the more persuasive the deeper the commitment. Before the commitment was firmly made, the costs of intervention were unknown and hypothetical; only the interests, seen in the light of global containment, seemed clear. After the commitment was made and expanded, the costs in Vietnam and at home became progressively clearer. By then the interests at stake had indeed grown, and the war could be abandoned only at considerable risk.

What, then, were the "lessons" of Vietnam as they relate to the policy that led to a war having such portentious consequences for American foreign policy? One apparent lesson was the difficulty of applying the precepts of a conventional—and conservative—statecraft to the policy of global containment, for the prudence of the one is not the prudence of the other. Nor can it be if the statesman is insistent upon seeing a seamless web of interests which, almost by definition, does not readily permit either careful discrimination between interests or equanimity over the prospect of occasional loss of interest.

Whether global containment is based on geopolitical considerations or on ideological grounds (it is compatible with either rationale), the result is the same. In either case, the reconciliation of interest and power must prove elusive. Whereas power is always limited, the interest in forming global containment is not. The ever threatening disparity between interest and power cannot be bridged by a mere act of will, a will that is ever triumphant because of the interest or purpose it reflects. Eventually, as was the case in Vietnam, the conviction of an ever triumphant will is bound to overtax power and to betray interest.

It is quite true that the past history of global containment does not bear out the claim by some of practice always conforming to principle. But that history does support the contention of a close correspondence. The burden of proof is reasonably placed on those who would contend that the global containment of the future might be expected to differ substantially from that of the past.

9

A policy of global containment would have to be conducted today in circumstances markedly less favorable than the circumstances of a generation ago. Even if we assume the restoration of a national will and consensus comparable to that of the 1950s and early 1960s, the point would remain that the overall relative advantage we once enjoyed could not be regained without a very considerable effort, and even then it could likely be regained only in part.

This will be apparent when we consider the military requirements of global containment. Whereas in the past this policy was undertaken from a position of strategic superiority, today and in the several years ahead it would have to be undertaken from at best a position of strategic parity or, more likely, from a slightly disadvantageous position. It is only reasonable to assume that a strenuous effort will be made to improve our strategic posture. It would be the height of imprudence not to make such effort, particularly if a policy of global containment were to be seriously entertained. That policy must presuppose either the retaining of a position of strategic superiority or, if strategic parity is the best that can be had, the achievement of conventional force capabilities that, in relation to Soviet forces, are superior to those maintained in the earlier period of containment. Without regaining the great asset we once enjoyed, containment cannot be prudently undertaken in the absence of parity in conventional forces, save perhaps where a distinctly favorable balance of interest may compensate for conventional inferiority.

A policy of global containment must rest on the assumption that we can and will regain an *overall* military position relative to the Soviet Union that is at least as favorable as the position we enjoyed a generation ago. Quite apart from the plausibility of this assumption, what might the Soviet Union be expected to do in the face of a policy that intends to resist its every move and that undertakes to develop the necessary means to do so? I am not speaking here of a policy intent on preserving interests outside this hemisphere that are indispensable to America's entire position in the world, such as the Persian Gulf. For the Soviet Union these interests are indispensable as the key to global predominance. The measures required to implement such a policy are not without risks. Confronted with even these measures, the Soviet leaders must anticipate the time when they will no longer enjoy their present military position. Moreover, they can have no assurance that, having once taken these measures, we will forego the temptation to achieve once again a position of strategic superiority. But if the risks inherent in the attempt to redress the present military balance are substantial, how much greater would they be if accompanied by a commitment to a policy of global containment?

In the present circumstances, a return to the expansive version of containment, if seriously intended, is likely to place us on the most dangerous of courses with the Soviet Union. This policy must convey the message to Moscow that the clock is to be set back at least 15 years, that the status of equality accorded the USSR by the late 1960s is henceforth to have a largely honorific significance, and that the United States no longer intends to accept the Soviet Union as a global power. Quite apart from the reaction of Soviet leaders to what they would see as a renewed determination to treat them as a regional power, what effect would this have on our principal allies?

If the experience of the past year or so is any indication,

the answer is reasonably clear. At best, it would further exacerbate the existing crisis in the Western alliance. At worst, it might lead to an open rupture and to the greatest diplomatic defeat for this country in the postwar period. Disagreement within the Atlantic alliance has almost always been greatest over issues that have not been specifically European. In truth, the alliance has seldom effectively functioned as an alliance with respect to these issues, even when the issue in question has vitally affected alliance interest. Of these, the energy crisis and ensuing differences over the proper Western policy to be pursued in the Middle East afford the most dramatic and important examples.

One may still argue that these differences have been largely the result of Western Europe's declining confidence in American leadership, discipline, and will, and that a resurgent America dedicated again to global containment would, in demonstrating these qualities, restore this badly impaired confidence. Without question, a more consistent and resolute American leadership would restore a measure of European confidence and elicit a greater degree of cooperation. It is, after all, scarcely surprising that given the character of American policy in recent years, Western Europe did not greet the hardened position toward the USSR in 1980 with enthusiasm. If this shift were to prove abortive, or if it were not to be followed up, America would risk losing a great deal. But Western Europe would risk losing everything.

In these circumstances, and with a vivid memory of the American record since the mid-1970s, what is surprising is that West European resistance to shifts in American policy during the Carter years was not more pronounced. At the same time, the effective reassertion of American power and leadership may yet prompt a quite different reaction, and sooner than is commonly expected. It will do so, however, only if the Europeans are persuaded that the United States is pursuing a policy that does not risk confrontation with the Soviet Union over interests deemed extraneous to the Western alliance. This task of persuasion has been difficult enough in the Middle East, where Western Europe's interests are manifest but where American policy has been seen to jeopardize those interests because of Washington's position on the Arab-Israeli conflict and — to a lesser degree — on the Soviet invasion of Afghanistan. Yet how much greater would European opposition be to a policy that, in seeking to deny the extension of Soviet power and influence in areas of little intrinsic concern to Western Europe, threatened to take Europe back to the conditions of the 1950s?

To the risks that a policy of global containment would likely incur must be added the costs. How great those costs would be, when added to those of a more moderate policy, is difficult to assess. Certainly they would be substantially greater, if only because a policy of global containment greatly increases the attractiveness of seeking to regain strategic superiority over the Soviet Union. They would also be substantially greater because this more ambitious policy holds out a greater promise of intervention and therefore requires the requisite conventional forces. It would be reckless to assume that interven-

167

tions in the future will prove less costly than those in the past. The Third World has not become more passive since the 1960s. Instead, it has become almost everywhere most resistant to superpower attempts to exercise the control or even the influence that was once part of the order of things.

The changes that have occurred in the Third World have raised the costs of intervention even in regions, such as Central America, where intervention in the past was almost effortless. A policy of global containment will no longer be able to rely on indirect methods or regional surrogates to the extent it relied on them in the past. These methods of implementing containment were scarcely an unqualified success in an earlier period. Today they appear less promising than before, given the rising assertiveness of most nations of the Third World, the instability that may overtake even the more reliable of those regimes on which global containment may depend, and the far greater military capability of the Soviet Union.

10

Could a policy of global containment be expected to command the necessary support at home? Could it elicit the domestic consensus required to sustain it over the long term? There are no easy answers to these questions. Yet they must be asked and in asking them we must have recourse to our past experience.

It is a commonplace that the policy of global containment enjoyed remarkable support among public and elites from its inception to Vietnam. It is also the case, however, that this consensus was dependent upon conditions that were unusually favorable. The period of global containment was attended by a domestic economy that suffered from virtually none of the difficulties that characterize the American economy today. The 1950s and early 1960s were virtually free from inflation. They were also years in which substantial economic growth appeared almost assured because of constant advances in technology and access to what seemed an inexhaustible source of cheap energy.

In these circumstances, foreign and defense policies claimed a proportion of the GNP that ranged from a high of 14 percent to a low of 9 percent. Yet it was not only a strong economic base and the expectation of continued prosperity that permitted devoting what in retrospect appears as so substantial a proportion of our wealth to support global containment. The America of this period was a society quite different from the society it was to become in the late 1960s and particularly in the 1970s. What is now termed the society of entitlements was then in a formative stage. By comparison with the demands presently made on government budgets, the demands made then were modest. Although it is quite true that even in the 1950s the conflict between defense spending and welfare programs was not unknown—witness the continuing debate that marked the years of the Eisenhower Administration—that conflict was modest by comparison with the conflict today.

The acceptance of the sacrifices entailed by global containment was also made possible by a society that accepted the primacy of foreign over domestic policy. This is only another way of saying that there was a remarkable national consensus in support of containment. It is easy to exaggerate the depth of the support afforded this policy and the resolution behind the commitment to its pursuance. In fact, containment was seriously tested in blood on one only occasion prior to Vietnam: Korea. But the Korean War was as much, if not more, an application of selective or moderate containment as it was of global containment. Put in different terms, the Korean intervention responded to the requirements of moderate containment though it was also the decisive event in the process that led to global containment.

It was the fear that the attack on South Korea, if left unopposed, might well eventuate in an armed attack on Western Europe that not only formed a principal motivation for our intervention, but also explains the relative absence of dissent to the Korean intervention. It was also the primacy of a conventional security interest, centered in Europe, that led to the extension of American containment policy to Asia. The wisdom of that extension did not pass unchallenged either then or in the following years. Yet as long as that extension was not put to the test by events, it was supported for more than a decade by what can only be termed a negative consensus. From the early 1950s to the mid-1960s, American commitments and policies remained relatively unchanged. Our bilateral and multilateral defense arrangements, now reflecting a policy of global containment, elicited some criticism by those who were persuaded that America had become overextended. In the absence of a serious test of policy, however, the criticism made little impact. Indeed, the successes enjoyed by American policy during these years, successes that were obtained largely by covert and indirect means, appeared to vindicate policy.

The years of global containment appeared to register a considerable foreign policy success, and they undeniably were successful. But that success rested on a fragile base. Eventually, one of our promissory notes, particularly one of our Asian notes, would have to be met, and by means that would put both policy and the consensus on which policy rested to a test even Korea had not represented. That the test of policy occurred in Vietnam was an unusual piece of bad luck. Still, those responsible for foreign policy are obliged to take the possibility of bad luck into their calculations. They cannot in prudence proceed on the assumption that a policy resting on no more than a negative consensus will never be seriously tested. In Vietnam, this negative consensus was put to such a test and its essential fragility laid bare.

When the question is asked whether a policy of global containment today could be expected to command the necessary support at home, it is not enough to point to the experience of an earlier period. Even if the circumstances of an earlier period could be approximately duplicated, they still would not support the case for returning to the policy of this period. (At least they do not do so unless it is assumed that a policy of global containment would now be able to avoid the kind of intervention we experienced in Vietnam.) Yet there is no apparent way by which this assumption can be made. On the contrary, the world in which global containment will have to be conducted appears to support a case for making the opposite assumption.

This being so, the risks of intervention, when measured in terms of domestic support, have increased. They have increased not because of the many, though dubious, "lessons" that have been drawn from our experience in Vietnam, but because of one indisputable lesson: success is the great solvent of serious public dissatisfaction over foreign policy, particularly over military intervention. Though difficult to justify from the outset, had the intervention in Vietnam succeeded within a relatively brief period, it is reasonable to assume that significant opposition to the war would not have arisen. Unless future interventions can find a justification in security interests that the public and the foreign policy elites find compelling, they will have to enjoy relatively quick and cheap success. Yet the prospects for satifying these requirements are less favorable than ever.

It is reasonably clear that the domestic support required for a return to the policy of a generation ago does not yet exist. Instead, in the emergence of a "new nationalism" we find a public that rejects the guilt and withdrawal of the post-Vietnam period, while being reluctant to embrace again the enthusiasms of the pre-Vietnam period. Though it has become strongly supportive of greater defense efforts, it has also remained cautious of the purposes for which American arms might be employed. Accordingly, though it is supportive of existing commitments, it has also remained cautious over endorsing new commitments — witness the less than overwhelming public response evoked by the Carter Doctrine.

The new nationalism appears thoroughly self-interested. It is precisely this trait that leads observers such as Podhoretz to conclude that the new nationalism lacks "a sense of things." Yet what it lacks is not an anticommunist disposition as such, but the anticommunist disposition of yesterday and the willingness of yesterday to act on the basis of that disposition.

Whether the prevailing public mood can be sustained remains to be seen. Expressing as it does an outlook supportive of a modest policy and based on calculations of self-interest, it is different from our experience since World War II. If, however, the new nationalism could be sustained, if it could avoid the disenchantment and withdrawal that followed Vietnam as well as the enthusiasm and involvement that preceded Vietnam, it would not need the intellectual guidance that some believe it must have. Indeed, the foreign policy elites might well benefit by taking their cue from the new nationalism rather than by endeavoring to instruct it. The essential elements of a viable consensus on foreign policy need not be further sought after. For the moment, they are apparent in the prevailing public mood.

It also remains to be seen whether the elites will accept

the self-interested outlook of the public as affording the broad guidelines within which a reformed foreign policy can be articulated and refined. They may not do so because some will regard the prevailing public outlook to lack the anticommunist disposition of yesterday, while others will find in this outlook a betrayal of the "internationalism" that enjoyed considerable favor in the foreign policy establishment during the preceding decade. Should this prospect materialize, the elites will be torn by dissension and an indispensable ingredient for an effective foreign policy will be missing.

11

If, however, a domestic consensus can be sustained in support of a policy of moderate containment, as outlined earlier in these pages, what is the great objection to its acceptance? Though described as moderate, it is not, after all, an inconsiderable enterprise. To redress the overall arms balance, to insure Western access to the oil supplies of the Persian Gulf, and generally to restore confidence abroad that America has the understanding and the discipline to maintain a solvent foreign policy, seems a substantial enough undertaking. Many observers believe that it will prove too much for us to undertake in our presently straitened economic condition. Even if this view is rejected, it is at least clear that the magnitude of the effort required to redress the overall arms balance, while markedly improving our military position in the Persian Gulf region, will place a heavy demand on an administration dedicated to achieving fiscal balance as rapidly as possible. Why, then, should we consider taking on more unless it can be shown that the more is essential to our security?

There is, of course, the interest in insuring access to nonfuel mineral supplies, without which the economies of the industrial democracies would be critically imperiled. In the case of this country, our dependence on imported minerals has grown in the past decade. Even so, we are still in a relatively favorable condition largely because the vast bulk of our imports come from developed and "safe" countries, Canada alone providing more than one-half of our needs. The one major supplier that may become unsafe is South Africa. In the foreseeable future, though, there seems little likelihood of serious interruptions in the supply of South African minerals. Moreover, in the case of chromium, the most important mineral we obtain from South Africa, a modest policy of stockpiling would reduce to bearable proportions a subsequent cutoff.

The position of our major allies, on the other hand, is much less favorable. While the import dependence of the United States on nonfuel minerals is moderate, with imports comprising about 15 percent of the total consumption, Western Europe and Japan are highly dependent on imports, with figures of 75 percent and 90 percent respectively. Even here the picture should not be overdrawn, since this dependency is substantially relieved by imports from other developed countries (Canada again being very important). Still, the remaining dependence on the developing states is considerable for both Western Europe and Japan. This dependency cannot be meaningfully compared to the case of oil. There is no Persian Gulf equivalent for nonfuel minerals, or even nearly so. This is not to say that the issue of Western access to nonfuel minerals of the developing world may thereby be dismissed. It is only to say that the prospects of a significant denial of imports to the industrial democracies are sufficiently modest as not to justify a policy of global containment.

These considerations bring us back to the difficult, perhaps insoluble, distinction between need and want. It is clear what we generally want to happen in the Third World (and it is the Third World that we are talking about). Yet it is also in much of the Third World that our distinction between need and want has often been the most tenuous, just as it is here that containment in the past has enjoyed the least success. The issue that a refurbished policy of global containment must raise is not whether it should be applied to those areas where need is apparent to all, as in the region of the Persian Gulf, but where it is plausible, at best, only if unverifiable assumption is piled upon unverifiable assumption.

The argument may be illustrated by reference to Central America, an area that is almost certain to provoke rising concern and controversy in the coming period. In

Central America there are no vital raw materials or minerals whose loss might provide the basis for legitimate security concerns. Yet Central America bears geographical proximity to the United States, and historically it has long been regarded as falling within our sphere of influence. As such, we have exercised the role great powers have traditionally exercised over small states that fall within their spheres of influence. We have regularly played a determining role in making and in unmaking governments, and we have defined what we have considered to be the acceptable behavior of governments. In Central America our pride is engaged as it cannot possibly be engaged in Africa or in Southeast Asia. If we do not apply a policy of a resurgent America to prevent the coming to power of radical regimes in Central America, we have even less reason to do so in other areas where conventional security interests are not apparent. Reasons of pride and historical tradition apart, it is here, if anywhere, that we enjoy clear military superiority and may expect to retain such superiority in the future. In Central America, then, one risk of an ambitious containment policy would be absent.

Would a return to a policy of the past work in Central America? Providing that we exercise some care in defining what we mean by "work," there is no persuasive reason for believing it would not. The measures required to insure success may prove unwelcome and embarrassing since we can have no assurance that indirect methods of intervention will prove sufficient. We have now passed the period of overthrowing an Arbenz in Guatemala, when disposing of governments to which we took offense was an easy undertaking. Today we must expect to deal with a more determined and effective opposition. The price promises to be markedly greater, and it will have to be paid in both the actions we take and in the reactions of others — particularly, though not only, in Latin America. It would be rash to assume that the assertion of our power will be met by the general response of a generation ago. In all likelihood, the experience of 1965, when we intervened in the Dominican Republic with the endorsement of the Organization of American States, cannot be repeated.

Moreover, the price to be paid for returning to a policy of the past cannot prudently be trimmed by halfway measures, that is, by an opposition to radical movements that still fails to prevent their taking power, or, more important, that fails to remove them should they achieve power. The result of such halfway measures will only be to create the conditions for another Cuba. Radical movements or radical regimes must be defeated. Yet even if we pay the necessary price for defeating them, we cannot be sure how long our success will endure. Success is likely to prove precarious because the defeated may well continue to enjoy broad support, and the victors will have to do what has to date apparently been impossible for them to do: enlist the support of centrist elements. Failing this support right-wing governments will have to be given steady outside support, even if this means the use of American forces.

It can be done. But why should we do it? If one replies that our security requires doing it, we still have to determine the nature of the security interests at stake. One presumably relates to Mexico. Is it reasonable to assume, however, that the course of Central America will seriously influence the course of Mexico? A positive response must presuppose that Mexican political stability is a quite fragile affair, else it is difficult to credit the view that Mexico's future will be materially affected by developments occurring in the small Central American states. The Mexican government has given no outward sign that these developments cause it serious concern. On the contrary, its public position is that if there is any real concern it is that the United States will revert to an openly interventionist policy in Central America to put down radical change rather than seeking to accommodate such change, while taking all possible measures to moderate it.

This public position, some observers have urged, is not to be taken at face value. It is only reflective of the need any Mexican government feels to take a position to the left of Washington and, more generally, to oppose interventionary measures by the American government. Why this need, however, to use Washington as a stalking horse for pursuing Mexico's true, though disavowed, interests? Does it reflect a serious weakness of the Mexican power structure or does it merely serve as a dispensable political convenience for the governing elite? If it is the former, then Mexican stability is indeed in for a difficult period ahead, and this quite apart from developments in Central America. If it is the latter, there is no apparent reason why we should respond to the Mexican government's convenience by taking on a burden that might well prove onerous. Mexico is quite capable of taking on this burden. A history of a century and more of resentment and complaint over the behavior of the colossus to the north can begin a new and overdue chapter.

There remains, it is true, the broader relationship-of-interests argument. If, it runs here, the Soviet Union observes our passivity to events in our own backyard that signal the loss of American control, what conclusions might it draw about our probable passivity in other, far more difficult, areas? The argument cannot simply be dismissed. Yet its persuasiveness depends, in the final reckoning, on what we do or fail to do in areas where vital interests are at stake. If we remain passive in these areas, what we do in Central America will have only marginal significance. The eagle that kills the deer in Central America will not frighten the bear in the Middle East.

It is not need that would prompt this course but want —a want, moreover, that the Soviet Union would not only accept but probably endorse, since it would be seen to help legitimize much of its own behavior. The only other coherent policy is to observe a hands-off position toward the events now occurring in Central America. Clearly, there are limits to such policy. We cannot distance ourselves from the internal strife of these states, if our doing so is interpreted either by the Soviet Union or by Cuba as an invitation to intervene on a significant scale. We cannot be expected to practice abstention in this region if others do not do so. This qualification, however, ought not to be used as an excuse for intervention in instances where the support of others can prove no more than marginal in determining the outcome. There is, unfortunately, no litmus test for determining what constitutes marginality and what does not. One evident test is the introduction of foreign combat forces; another is the supply of weapons on such a scale that a government cannot match it without receiving a substantial infusion of arms. Admittedly of a general nature, these guidelines are still not without utility. In the case of Nicaragua, for example, it is reasonably clear that it was not the outside help given the insurgents that finally tipped the balance in their favor. The Somoza government did not suffer from lack of arms. It *was* dealt a critical psychological blow by the withdrawal of American support. But this is quite another matter.

Where Central American governments are not placed at a serious disadvantage by outside intervention, we should stand aside from internal strife. If by doing so further radical regimes should come to power, we would accept the outcome. We would also give them reason to maintain a normal relationship with the Soviet Union, rather than to follow in the footsteps of Cuba. Such inducement, of which the economic aid given to Nicaragua in 1980 forms an example, may be seen as a mere euphemism for blackmail. I have no objection to the term. Blackmail is a commonplace in the relations of states. Having put up with the spectacular instances of it that we have seen in the past decade, to balk here would truly be a case of straining at the gnat while swallowing the camel.

If we were instead to swallow the gnat, and perhaps a few others as well in the years to come, it would not signify that we liked this diet. It would only mean that we recognized at last that we are in a position where we can afford to view changes we do not welcome with the equanimity they deserve.

What we cannot view with equanimity is the states of Central America entering into a relationship with either the Soviet Union or its proxy, Cuba, that resembles the relationship between the Soviet Union and Cuba. Geographical proximity has not lost its significance. At issue, then, is not whether Central America continues to form a part of this nation's sphere of influence. Instead, it is the nature of the influence we should seek to exercise within our sphere and how such influence may best be preserved. There is a clear difference in principle between those who define our sphere of influence to include the internal order of states and those who do not. The difference ought not to be confused with the preeminently practical judgment on the policy best suited to prevent the kind of intrusion by an outside power we should aim to prevent.

The view taken here will satisfy neither those who want to prevent the emergence of radical regimes (whatever their relationship to the Soviet Union or Cuba) by supporting the status quo, nor those who urge the course of reform in order to prevent radical movements from arising in the first place. From both of these perspectives, the critical problem for American foreign policy is how to deal with the internal order, for deal with it we presumably must. To supporters of the status quo, we have neither the wisdom and understanding nor the means to effect desirable change. Attempts to reform the status quo therefore run the risk of making an admittedly imperfect situation much worse by creating instability and thereby opening the way to radical regimes. To supporters of reform, it is only through promoting needed change that we can contain the appeal to radical solutions and augment the strength of nonradical, though progressive, forces.

These contrasting views go back to the years preceding the Alliance for Progress. Although the argument is as inconclusive today as it was a generation ago, the record of American foreign policy — whether in Latin America or elsewhere in the developing world — does not provide much support for those who continue to urge our role as reformer of governments and societies. To say this is not to endorse the status quo argument, which is quite as intent upon determining the internal order as are the reformers. It is to say that we should pursue a policy that, so far as it is even barely consonant with our security interests, eschews the role of influencing the internal order of others.

There are evidently limits to this counsel. In the case of the Central American states, one cannot advocate blanket abstention from attempting to influence the internal order while also advocating inducements to emergent radical regimes in order that they not follow in the footsteps of Cuba. But surely there is a very considerable difference between the nature and scope of the would-be influence such inducements represent and the nature and scope of the influence sought by those who would either support the status quo or push for pervasive reform.

The general policy suggested here is not without defects. One defect, as already noted, is that it depends upon criteria the nature of which leave a substantial gray area of uncertainty. Viron P. Vaky criticizes this approach by noting that "it would involve the United States only at the most deteriorated and dangerous point, when a Soviet threat was unambiguously clear and the only option left was intervention."* This danger, however, would arise not so much from the admittedly residual uncertainty attending the policy as from the reluctance of an administration to apply it at all. There is no need to wait until this extreme point in time. Indeed, almost any policy may be criticized in this manner. Vaky also notes, in

---

*Viron P. Vaky, "Hemispheric Relations: 'Everything is Part of Everything Else,'" *Foreign Affairs*, (*America and the World;* 1980), p. 642.

criticism, that the view taken here considers internal conflict and revolutionary changes "exclusively through the East-West prism." But if our concern is security how else should we view such conflict and change? It is quite another matter, however, to argue that within this context we must assume either a pro-American or pro-Soviet (or pro-Cuban) outcome. This is indeed the assumption on which many would base an interventionary policy today, but is not the assumption on which the argument advanced here is based. By contrast, the policy advocated in these pages has a clear and limited focus. It restricts our attempts to influence the internal order within the narrowest of bounds compatible with our security interests. It does not presume that we know what is best for others, but only what is necessary to satisfy our minimal interests.

In the Central American case, our claims are rooted in geography and history. If these claims ought not to extend to the internal order of states here, there is still less reason for extending them elsewhere in the Third World. The strictures made earlier with respect to the Persian Gulf do not contradict this conclusion. In the Gulf, we are necessarily concerned with internal order because this issue cannot be separated from a vital interest in access to oil supplies. The same vital interest bids us oppose the extension of Soviet influence in that region. Were it not for this interest, we could view changes in the internal order and the extension of Soviet influence with the relative detachment that holds out the best promise of avoiding the excesses that have characterized American foreign policy in the past.

12

There is no fate that decrees we must repeat these excesses of concern and withdrawal. Having experienced the consequences of both in the past two decades, we ought to have learned that the result of both is to lead to the insolvency of policy. A period of withdrawal and of passivity has come to an end. If it is to be succeeded by a period of America everywhere resurgent and activist, we will risk jeopardizing those interests that are critical to the nation's security and well-being.

The restoration of those interests will prove no small task, especially if it cannot be undertaken with the cooperation of our principal allies. This cooperation is far from assured, and there is no reliable way by which it can be assured in the circumstances that have characterized the Western alliance in recent years. These circumstances, it has long been apparent, dictate that one great object of American foreign policy ought to be the restoration of a more normal political world, a world in which those states possessing the elements of great power again play the independent role their power entitles them to play. Without such restoration there may well be no escape from a return to a policy of global containment. The logic of this policy does not come so much from the specific conflicts of interest arising between the Soviet Union and the United States, important as these conflicts undoubtedly are, as it does from the temptations — if not the compulsions — of a system that still retains so markedly bipolar a character. It is the essential structural features of the conflict that must account for both its persistence and its pervasiveness. Until such time as these structural features are substantially moderated, the argument for global containment, whatever the criticism made of it, will have a persuasiveness that has to be reckoned with.

The structural features cannot be moderated so long as potential power does not find its full expression in the political-military as well as the economic sphere. So long as states possessing the elements of great power refuse to play the role their power entitles them to play, and so long as they are not seriously urged or even pushed into doing so, there can be no satisfactory resolution to the issues dealt with here. In the case of our principal allies, the disparity between latent and actual power has grown. If not substantially reduced, the disparity is almost certain to lead to still greater difficulty in alliance relationships, and this quite apart from the manner in which America conducts its foreign policy.

The principal difficulty that characterizes alliance relationships today goes much deeper than issues of style or even of substance. It reflects the frustration and resentment of those who are now able to assume responsibility for their security but have yet to do so. If they were at long last to do so, the political world as we know it would be transformed. A third of a century after World War II, that transformation is surely long overdue.

About the Author

ROBERT W. TUCKER is professor of political science at both the Johns Hopkins University and the Johns Hopkins School of Advanced International Studies in Washington. He is a graduate of the U.S. Naval Academy and received his M.A. and Ph.D. from the University of California in 1946–49. He has been at Johns Hopkins since 1954. He has also served as a member of the staff of the Naval War College and as a consultant to the Department of State and the Department of Defense. He is a trustee and co-director of studies at the Lehrman Institute.

Professor Tucker has lectured widely throughout the United States on American foreign policy generally and on a number of specific topics including, most recently, the Middle East. He is the author of *The Just War: A*

Study in Contemporary American Doctrine (The Johns Hopkins Press, 1960); *Force, Order, and Justice* [co-author, with Robert E. Osgood] (The Johns Hopkins Press, 1967); *Nation or Empire? The Debate over American Foreign Policy* (The Johns Hopkins Press, 1968); *The Radical Left and American Foreign Policy* (The Johns Hopkins Press, 1971); *A New Isolationism: Threat or Promise?* (Universe Books, 1972); *The Inequality of Nations* (Basic Books, 1977); and *The Fall of the First British Empire and the Origins of the American Revolution (1763–1775)* (forthcoming, The Johns Hopkins Press).

He is also the author of numerous articles. Among the most recent are: "America in Decline: The Foreign Policy of 'Maturity,'" *Foreign Affairs,* January 1980; "American Power and the Persian Gulf," *Commentary,* November 1980; and "The Purposes of American Power," *Foreign Affairs,* December 1980.